Candle Decorating

By the Same Author

Kitchen Candlecrafting

Candle Decorating

Ruth Monroe

South Brunswick and New York: A. S. Barnes and Company
London: Thomas Yoseloff Ltd

A. S. Barnes and Co., Inc.
Cranbury, New Jersey 08512

Thomas Yoseloff Ltd
108 New Bond Street
London W1Y OQX, England

Library of Congress Cataloging in Publication Data

Monroe, Ruth.
  Candle decorating.

  1. Candles. I. Title.
TT896.5.M64   745.59′3   73-3171
ISBN 0-498-01281-6

Printed in the United States of America

Contents

5

Introduction

Just before completing this book, I attended my first gift show and was pleasantly surprised at the number of exhibitors displaying candles. On closer inspection I was even more surprised that many of the candles were displayed at all. Some of the ideas and designs were creative, original, and showed much imagination and talent, but the execution of these promising candles left much to be desired. It wasn't possible to determine whether the poor quality of the candles was due to lack of pride in workmanship or to lack of knowledge of the craft. In any event, candles that could have been great were only mediocre.

Home candlecrafting is in its infancy, but interest in this art form is growing at a tremendous pace. It is a totally fascinating activity, regardless of whether it is a leisure-time activity or a hardheaded business project.

Like any other craft, however, it takes some time and a number of mistakes for one to become proficient. Anyone can thread a mold, dump in some wax, and call himself a candlemaker. But only those willing to experiment and to constantly strive for improvement can call themselves craftsmen. No matter how good his product, the real craftsman is always a little dissatisfied. He keeps pursuing perfection although he knows it to be the most elusive of goals.

If you want to sell your candles, it is my firm belief that an increasingly quality-conscious buying public will recognize excellence in workmanship and make its purchases accordingly. However, if you are more interested in making candles for the sheer joy of creating, a well-made candle is infinitely more pleasing and soul-satisfying than an inferior one.

Goofs in candlemaking are probably less expensive to correct than in any other craft. Merely throw your mistakes back in the melting pot and start all over. With the proper materials, good candles are not more difficult, time consuming, or expensive to make than poor ones, so why settle for something second rate?

Candle Decorating

1
Basic Candlemaking

Many letters have been received asking why there are no books that give exact proportions and eliminate all the guesswork in making candles. Why can't a book be written, for example, that would state "for a mold twelve inches tall and three inches in diameter so many pounds of wax, so much additive, and X-size wick should be used"? Such a book would be the easiest thing in the world to write and it would be totally worthless.

The composition, degree of quality control, and refining of waxes vary so greatly between different companies and even within the same companies that the first problem encountered is with the waxes. Waxes from various companies with the same melting point can be vastly different in their burning qualities because of their hardness, degree of refinement, and so on. Some of the microcrystalline waxes have a very high melting point but are quite plastic and malleable, whereas the high-melting-point paraffins are usually extremely hard and brittle.

Then there are literally dozens of additives, including the micro waxes, and when they are combined with the paraffin waxes generally used in making candles, the end results are all different. Some of the differences are slight and some are quite drastic. All of these things have as much bearing on the type and kind of wick to be used as does the diameter of the candle.

Another problem that arises when giving directions to use a certain size wick in a certain size candle is the question of what is expected of the candle when it burns. Should it drip, should all the wax be consumed with a minimum of dripping, or should it be a well-burning candle?

Candle Decorating

As you can see from the above, there is no one way to make a candle. That is why it is necessary for each person to experiment and keep records of test candles to determine exactly what type of wax, additive, and wick works best for a particular purpose.

It is also why there is no way to write a book that could give specific directions without making tests of combinations of every wax, additive, and wick size on the market. Unfortunately, all any candle book can do is give general instructions on candlemaking. Then it is up to you to take these instructions and refine them to meet your own needs and standards.

Since detailed instructions for making various kinds of candles were given in another book, and since this is primarily a candle decorating and not a candlemaking book, the making of candles will be touched on only briefly.

Unless it is bought in a craft shop in small quantities, wax usually comes in cartons containing five slabs weighing approximately ten or eleven pounds each. These slabs can be easily broken into small pieces by hitting them with a hammer.

The melting and pouring pot can be any leak-proof, heat-proof container with a handle and pouring spout. Wax pieces should be put in the pot and placed in a pan of water over medium heat until the wax has melted. Don't place the wax over direct heat and don't leave the melting wax unattended.

If any of the various plastics, such as "crystals," are used as an additive, heat them separately in a small amount of wax. More heat is required to melt the plastic particles than is necessary for melting wax. Therefore, the plastic should be melted and then added to the wax. If stearic acid is used, it may be put directly into the melting pot. Beeswax or the micro waxes may also be added to the wax as it melts.

Dyes are available in solid, powder, or liquid form. For the beginner and those making candles in small quantitiees, the dye buds are probably the best. If many candles are to be made, the powdered dye is more economical in the long run. This type of dye is sold in lots of one pound or more and can be added to the wax in the powder form or made into dye buds. Adding liquid dye drop by drop is probably the most convenient method of duplicating a particular shade time after time.

Dye should be added to the melted wax when it reaches pouring temperature and then stirred thoroughly to be certain it is well mixed with the wax. After stirring, let the wax sit for a couple of minutes so that the bubbles caused by the stirring will have a chance to dissipate. Dye should be added in small amounts until the desired color is obtained. By placing a few drops of the colored wax in a bowl of cold water or on a white plate or saucer, it is possible to get an approximate idea of the color of the finished candle.

Scent or perfume must have an oil base to mix well with wax, and it should also be added just before pouring. It may also be added to the wax that is used for refilling.

A wax fire is only a remote possibility, but should one occur, never use water to quench it. Cover the flame with a pot lid or sprinkle baking soda over the flame. One of the commonest causes of wax fires is failure to keep the outside of the melting pot wiped clean. Any wax left on the outside of the container will melt and run down into the stove burner.

While the wax is melting, assemble your mold for pouring. Thread the wick through the hole in the bottom of the metal mold, pull it through the mold, and fasten it at the top to the metal wick rod that comes with each mold. Pull the wick taut and insert the screw in the wick hole. Wind the wick around the screw two or three times and then fasten the screw securely in the hole. Cut the wick so that about half an inch is left by the screw. Place mold sealer around the screw and wick. Center the wick at the top of the mold before pouring.

As added protection against leakage from the wick hole, half-inch squares can be cut from old inner tubes. Punch holes in the center of the squares and thread the wick through them before inserting it in the wick hole. Very seldom will any wax leak from the bottom if a couple of the squares are placed snugly against the bottom of the mold, and the screw placed through the holes in the squares, then fastened in the wick hole.

Sometimes the screw is bypassed completely, and two or three of the rubber squares are used with a slip knot tied in the bottom of the wick to hold it in place. If this method is used, the knot must be pulled very tightly against the rubber squares on the bottom of the mold. When either of these techniques is used, mold sealer is unnecessary.

When the mold is threaded and the wax has reached the correct pouring temperature, warm the mold. This can be done by inserting the hose from a hair dryer in the mold, holding the mold under hot running water or placing it in a low oven. If the mold is warmed with water, be sure that no water gets inside the mold. Too much heat in the oven will melt the solder on molds, and so the safest procedure here is to heat the oven and then turn it off before putting the molds in. A more expensive way to warm the molds is to use a heat gun.

When pouring hot wax into a mold, always have some protection between the hand and the mold. Although the molds can be held with a hot pad or something similar, the larger ones are hard to grip and have a tendency to slip. I have found that the best solution to this problem is to wrap a small towel around the mold, twist the ends together, and hold the ends of the towel while pouring the wax. Tilt the mold and pour the hot wax slowly down the inside. Pouring too rapidly will result in bubbles, which will wind up as pit marks on the surface of the candle. Fill candle to within one inch of the top of mold.

The water bath container can be anything wider and taller than the mold. Large plastic wastebaskets make great vats for the water bath. Fill the container with lukewarm water until it reaches a level about one inch lower than the top of the mold. Grasp the top of the filled mold with a hot pad and lower it into the water. Wax hardens from the sides of the mold first, and when there is a film of congealed wax about one-fourth of an inch thick around the sides of the mold and a depression has formed in the center of the candle, the mold can be removed from the water.

Unless the candle is refilled with hot wax, there will be a deep indentation in its bottom and holes throughout the middle of it. The candle can be refilled by poking holes around the wick and repacking them with hot wax the same color as the candle. The refilling may have to be done as many as three or four times to make certain that all cavities are filled. By doing this you have a solid wax candle and not a piece of Swiss cheese.

Use a high melting point wax (160–165°) for hurricane candles and never burn them for more than two or three hours at a time. Medium-melting-point-wax (143–150°) is best for pillar candles, and a low-melting-point-wax (128–130°) makes better container candles.

The proper wax temperature for pouring into metal molds is between 180° and 200°. If the temperature of the wax is much higher, there is likely to be a problem with dye discoloration since some dyes cannot tolerate extreme heat.

For pouring wax into glass containers, heat the glass and pour at 165° to 180°. Some glass can stand more heat than others, and it will be necessary to experiment to find the correct temperature for the particular glass being used. Since hot wax poured into a cold glass container will crack the glass, the glass should always be warmed.

Hurricane candles are made without a wick but, during pouring they are treated just as any other candle. When a film has formed on the inside edge of the mold about one-fourth of an inch thick, pour the liquid wax out of the mold. This will leave a thin wax shell. The inside of this shell will probably be rough, but it can be smoothed by filling the shell with hot wax and then pouring it out immediately. A hole should be cut in the bottom of the candle while it is still soft and in the mold.

When the shell is removed, it will be necessary to smooth the top edge of the candle on a hot surface.

A deep-fat thermometer from the dime store serves very adequately as a thermometer for wax. This is an investment I strongly recommend because the wax temperature can be very important to a well-made, beautiful candle.

Wax cools slowly, and it generally takes about eight hours before a candle can be removed from a metal mold. Remove the screw from the bottom of the mold and turn the mold upside down. The candle should slide out gently but if it doesn't, gently tap the top of the mold onto a towel which has been folded several times. If this doesn't work, place the mold in the refrigerator until the outside of the mold is cold to the touch. Leaving the candle in the refrigerator for too long a period will usually result in a cracked candle. Clean, lint-free molds and the occasional use of a mold release will facilitate easy release and help to obtain unblemished candle surfaces.

Once the candle is removed from the mold, the seam line along the side should be trimmed with a sharp knife and the bottom leveled. The leveling can be done on any flat surface that is hot enough to melt the wax. An electric skillet makes an excellent leveling pan.

When a candle is poured in a mold without a hole in the bottom for threading the wick, such as a bowl or a glass, it is necessary to insert the wick after the candle is poured. One way to do this is to punch a hole in the center of the candle after the wax is firm, but before it becomes hard. An ice pick or a piece of coat hanger makes short work of this job. If the candle hardens before the hole is made, heat an ice pick and melt a hole through the candle.

A wire core wick is less trouble to insert into a hole than a braided wick, but a braided wick can be dipped in hot wax to make it more rigid and easier to thread. As the wax cools, strip the waxed wick between thumb and forefinger to straighten it and place the wick in the hole.

A metal wick tab or holder is also useful for holding the wick in molds where there is no wick hole. The wick tab is extensively used when making container candles. Place the wire core wick in the hole in the center of the tab and push the prongs around it so that it is gripped firmly. Put the wick tab in the center of the mold and pour in about half an inch of wax. When the wax has hardened, pull the wick straight and fasten it to a rod across the top of the container to hold it in place. The filling of the mold can then be completed.

When a wick is placed in a hole, it must be sealed so that it will remain in the candle. On some candles the bottom can be covered with clay or mold sealer and hot wax poured down the wick hole. An eye dropper is an excellent instrument for getting wax into the hole without splashing it all over the rest of the candle. Another way is to touch a hot ice pick or an electric needle to the wax around the wick at the bottom and top of candle.

2
Terms, Tips, and Trivia

This chapter is more or less a reference chapter. It seemed to be a simple solution to the problem of endless repetition that would otherwise be necessary. It also solves the problem of where to put useful miscellaneous information that has no place in the balance of the book.

SCULPTURING OR SOFT WAX

Where used in this book, sculpturing or soft wax means any pliable, plastic wax. These waxes are not necessarily low-melting-point waxes since some of the plastic microcrystallines have a melting point of 175°. A soft wax can be beeswax, sculpturing wax, some microcrystallines, or a combination of these waxes.

All of them need to be warmed to some extent to make them pliable enough to bend without breaking. They can be melted and then used as they harden. Small amounts can be warmed in hot water or even from the heat of your hands. Larger pieces can be put out in the sun for a short time.

SODIUM SILICATE

Water glass, as sodium silicate is often called, is a flame-proofing liquid available at most drugstores. It should be used with all flammable decorating materials which might come in contact with the candle flame.

Decorations can be brushed or dipped, and if brushes are cleaned before the liquid hardens, they can be cleaned with water.

Candle Decorating

CORE CANDLE

A core candle is a candle that becomes the center of a larger candle. Its primary use is for the floral fantasy candles, ice cube candles, and some chunk candles. A core candle is usually no more than an inch in diameter, and often a taper serves as a core.

CONTAINER CANDLE

This is any candle that is poured and burned in the same container. Containers are usually made of class.

HURRICANE CANDLE

Actually, this is not a candle at all but a shell of wax inside which a votive candle is burned. Hurricane candles last indefinitely because they are not consumed by a flame. Only the votive candle burns and it is replaced as needed.

VOTIVE CANDLE

A very small, often-scented candle which is used with hurricane candles or can be burned as a candle by itself.

INSTANT WAX

Instant wax is useful for making container candles without the bother of heating and pouring wax. These are small granules of hard wax which are poured around a wick in a glass container. Because of the amount of air between the pieces of wax, it does not make a particularly long-burning candle, but it does make a candle.

You may buy this product or make your own by grating a piece of slab wax. If desired, it can be colored and scented before grating, but if you have to melt the wax to add the dye and scent, you might as well pour the hot wax into the container and have a good candle. However, this is a fine way to get rid of leftover wax that has already been colored or scented. If you sell supplies, it can be packaged in plastic bags with a length of wick and a tab and sold along with a glass container as a candlemaking kit.

FIRE STARTERS

Another way to use leftover wax. Mix hot wax with sawdust or shredded paper and as the wax hardens, spoon it out onto squares of waxed paper. Roll the waxed paper around the wax and twist the ends of the paper to fasten. Small ones are great for starting a charcoal fire, and the larger ones will soon have the logs in the fireplace burning merrily.

X-ACTO KNIVES

These little jewels are almost indispensable when working with candles. They can cut wick, trim seam lines, and handle many other chores. The blunt end of the handle makes an excellent tool for pushing pins into candles, or it can also be used as an aid in removing some castings from ceramic molds. The new electric ones now on the market promise to be of even more assistance to the candlemaker. These knives are available at all hobby shops and hardware stores.

CRAZING OR CRACKLING

Crazing or crackling on a candle usually sends it back to the melting pot, but sometimes this particular finish is wanted. To deliberately craze a candle, pour the candle in the usual manner and then pour out the center wax after a coating has formed around the sides of the mold. Let the wax cool for a while and then place mold in the refrigerator until cold. Fill the cavity with hot wax, and when the candle is removed from the mold, the outer coating will be a mass of cracks.

The crazed pattern can be emphasized by covering the candle with a coat of antiquing paint and then wiping it down. The paint will remain in the cracks but can be wiped off the rest of the candle.

MOTTLING

Mottling is something else that most candlemakers try to avoid in their candles. Mottles in wax look like white bubbles, and most wax is mottled to some extent when you buy it. The mottled effect can be quite attractive in some instances, and it can be accentuated by the addition of oil to the wax before it is poured. If heavy mottling is desired, don't add anything to the wax such as stearic or crystals which will make the wax opaque. The more opaque the wax, the less visible the mottling.

BLUE DYE

Do not overheat any wax containing blue dyes or other colors which contain blues such as green or purple. Too much heat will cause the dye to discolor either at the time of heating or within a short time thereafter.

BLACK DYE

Black candles are a problem because often the excessive amount of dye needed to make a truly black candle affects the burning qualities of the candle. When making a black candle, don't begin with clear wax. Collect all your scrap wax and throw it into the melting pot. If you have a number of colors, the result is likely to be some shade of brown, but this will give a good base for adding black. If there isn't any scrap wax available, add a dark blue dye to clear wax and then add the necessary amount of black dye. Both of these methods will cut down considerably on the amount of black dye needed.

PLASTER MOLDS

Plaster molds should be treated before pouring wax into them in order to prevent sticking. The cavity of the mold may be painted with thinned, heat-resistant varnish and the mold oiled each time before use.

Another method is to soak the mold in a thin oil such as automobile transmission fluid for several hours. No further treatment is required after this. Even after treating a mold, the wax will stick unless it is poured at a low temperature.

THOMAS REGISTER

If you need a certain product and don't know where to find it or if you can't find something locally and need a source of supply, check the Thomas Register in the reference department of the local library. These books give the names and addresses of the major manufacturers in the U.S. under the product listing. For instance, if you want to find a source of wax, look under Waxes and then find the particular type of wax needed under a subheading, such as Paraffin, Beeswax, and so on.

TELEPHONE DIRECTORIES

Most libraries also have telephone directories for the larger cities in the country. The Yellow Pages of these directories can be very helpful in locating suppliers.

ROASTER OVEN

For someone who wants to melt twenty or thirty pounds of wax at one time, and particularly for the person who works and has to do his candlemaking at night, an electric roaster oven can be one of the best things that ever happened. These ovens were very popular several years ago for cooking turkeys, large roasts, and such, and they can often be bought secondhand at a small price by checking the ads in the newspaper and sometimes at secondhand stores.

The oven has a heat control that permits setting at a certain temperature, and that temperature will be maintained for an indefinite period. There is a separate pan inside the heating unit that is easily removed so that all the wax can be poured out. Cleaning is a snap. Just melt the wax remaining in the pan and wipe with a paper towel.

For the person who works, the pan may be filled with wax chunks in the morning before leaving. If the temperature is set between 175° and 200°, the wax will be melted and ready for pouring when he returns from the office. The heat can then be raised to the desired temperature and the hot wax transferred to a pouring container and used as is, or the melting pot can be filled and placed on a stove burner for a short time to raise the temperature of the wax.

DECORATING

Much time can be saved in describing the methods of decorating individual candles if instructions such as "attach candle to base" or "flameproof decorations" are not repeated for each candle to which they apply. To avoid this repetition, some decorating techniques are listed below. Then when you see the picture of a candle and the instructions for decorating it, if it has a base or flammable decorations, you will know how to handle these things. If this section is read carefully, it will fill in any blanks that seem to exist in the decorating instructions.

WHIPPED WAX

Whipped wax is made by whipping partially cooled wax with a fork or eggbeater. Allow wax to cool until it has filmed over and then whip briskly. Beat the wax until a thick froth forms on the top, skim off the froth, and apply to the candle. Continue whipping and skimming until the wax hardens. If the wax is whipped until it is dry, it will not stick to the candle.

Whipped wax is used for attaching decorations, for a snow effect, or as a decoration itself. The low-melting-point wax is preferable because it whips up with a much softer texture than the harder waxes. Also, the low melting point wax is quite tacky and far superior to hard waxes for fastening decorations securely.

Lay the candle flat when applying large areas of whipped wax to its side. If wax is put on an upright candle, it will slide toward the bottom.

Whipped wax is usually applied in small sections so that decorations can be inserted before the wax hardens. If you see instructions stating "cover base of candle with whipped wax," this means just what it says, but it also means to cover only the amount of space at one time that can easily be worked before the wax hardens. When one area is completed, move on to an adjacent section and proceed in this manner until the entire base is covered.

WHIP WAX

This material should not be confused with whipped wax although it is also whipped. Whip Wax is the trade name of a commercial product which is sold in a liquid form. No heat is used with it, and after it is whipped, it can be applied with your fingers if you wish.

After beating with a rotary beater, Whip Wax assumes a soft, fluffy appearance and is about the consistency of cake frosting. In fact, if you are adept at using a cake-decorating tool, you can decorate a candle just as you would a cake. The texture of Whip Wax is much finer than that obtained by whipping regular wax.

Food colors may be used for dyes. They may be added before beating for a solid color throughout the wax, or they may be added after wax is whipped for a streaked effect. Whip Wax is water soluble, and utensils can be cleaned with water after use.

The wax stays workable for two or three hours, which gives it a definite advantage over whipped wax in many decorating situations. Drying time is rather long, and the completed candle should be set aside for several days before it is handled.

Whip Wax is generally available wherever candle supplies are sold. If you can't find anyone who stocks it, write to American Wax Corporation, Box F, Azusa, California 91702.

TEXTURING

Texturing covers a multitude of decorating techniques. Basically, it means altering the surface of a candle by adding to it or by removing from it a portion of the surface. Even adding whipped wax is a form of texturing. Wax can be stippled on by dipping crumpled paper towels into partially cooled or slightly whipped wax and touching the towel to the candle. Dripping wax down the sides of the candle is another method of texturing.

A texturing technique that provides colorful and unusual candles is loading the end of a knife or spatula with partially cooled wax and smashing it against the side of a candle. Press the wax firmly against the candle so that it will stick, but don't try to get it too smooth. Part of this candle's attraction is its rough surface.

A variation of this texturing technique is to put the gobs of wax on the inside of the mold before the candle is poured. If this method is used, remember that the harder the wax that is pressed against the mold, the less likely it is to melt when hot wax is poured in. Some melting improves the appearance of the finished candle, but there should be definite patches of the original colors. This candle provides an interesting study in contrasts because the surface of colored globs of wax will be rough and full of holes while the poured surface will be smooth.

Reverse texturing can be done by carving or scraping the sides of the candle with a comb, steel brush, steel wool, or even a saw. A ball peen hammer makes interesting dents in a candle, and you might also try tapping soft drink bottle caps into the wax in interlocking designs.

The texturing possibilities are limitless, and texturing offers one way to salvage a candle with a less-than-perfect surface. Often a textured candle will be more attractive than one with a satin finish.

TOOLING

Tooling can also be considered a form of texturing but in a more orderly form. For this it is necessary to have a set of the metal tools made for leather work. The designs on the tools are transferred to the wax by placing the tools against the candle and tapping with a hammer. All sorts of patterns and designs can be worked out using these tools, and they may also be used in conjunction with other types of decorating. The designs can be made to stand out more if they are rubbed with one of the paste metallic paints such as Treasure Gold or Rub 'n Buff.

ADHESIVE

When used in connection with candles, adhesive refers to one of the sticky, putty-like substances that comes in a roll. Wholesale florists have some good adhesives, and other excellent ones that are used for caulking can be found in most hardware stores. These adhesives stick to wax and will hold light decorations very satisfactorily. Just take a small piece of adhesive, place it on the back of the decoration, and press it against the candle.

ATTACHING DECORATIONS WITH PINS

Always use gold sequin pins for lightweight gold decorations and silver sequin pins for silver decorations. Regular sewing pins should be used for heavier decorations. If possible, try to position decorations in such a manner that they overlay and conceal the pinheads. When this is not possible, cover all pinheads with a drop of hot wax. Pins may be pushed into the candle with the end of an X-Acto knife handle.

BASES

Unless a contrasting base is needed, pour base at the same time candle is poured. This will eliminate the need to try to match wax colors if a base is needed later. Cake pans, pie tins, bowls, or salad molds are a few of the items suitable for base molds.

Styrofoam is used extensively as a base for candles, and it will benefit from a few wax dips. Dipping a styrofoam base until it has a good wax coat results in a more professional looking candle.

Candles can be attached to bases very snugly by the use of wire or small nails with no heads. If wire is used, cut three lengths about one inch long. Using pliers, push the wire or nail into the bottom of the candle about half way. Press the candle onto the base so the other half of the wire tips are embedded in the base. Dip base in hot wax just to the bottom of the candle. The hot wax will run between the base and candle for a good seal and a smooth connection.

DIPPING FLOWERS

The appearance of most plastic, paper, and cloth flowers is greatly improved by a dunking in hot wax. Dip flowers one at a time and shake off excess wax onto newspapers. Use the low-melting-point wax for dipping to reduce the possibility of wax flaking off of the flowers after it has hardened.

ATTACHING DECORATIONS

Decorations may be attached to a candle with pins, glue, adhesive, whipped wax, hot wax, or an electric needle or soldering gun. For heavy flowers, dig a small hole in the candle where the flower is to fit and melt wax in the hole with a hot ice pick or electric needle. Push the short stem of the flower into the hole immediately, and it will be held firmly when the wax hardens. When using an electric pencil or soldering gun for attaching decorations, a light touch is the secret of success. Too much pressure or lingering too long one one spot will result in an excessive amount of wax melting away.

PAINT

Oil paints have always been the best paints for candles, but the extended drying time made them impractical. There are now on the market oil paintsticks which look like huge crayons. These can be thinned with turpentine the same as tube oils, and they dry in a short time. Also, they can be used straight from the stick for highlighting without the addition of turpentine and dry in minutes. With the paintsticks, you get the coverage of the regular oils and almost the drying time of acrylics.

ASSEMBLING WAX FIGURES

Some figures from plaster molds come in sections, and it is necessary to join these sections to form a complete figure. Trim the mold seams and apply low-melting-point wax to the pieces to be joined. This can be done by brushing hot wax on the two sections of the casting or by holding the brush between the sections and drawing it out as they are joined together. Brush hot wax around the joining line and then dip.

CASTINGS

Used as a verb, casting means pouring. Casting a mold is the same thing as pouring into a mold. Used as a noun, casting is the finished object removed from the mold.

ANTIQUING

Antiquing can be done with a variety of paints, but I believe the best of the antiquing paints are sold by ceramic shops. If you have a wax figurine you don't want to paint, a coat of antiquing liquid and a wipe down with a soft cloth will bring out all the detail as well as adding a mellowness that the shiny wax doesn't have. Too-bright colors can be toned down with an overcoat of antiquing paint.

Special solvents are necessary for cleaning brushes used for antiquing. If it is not desired to have an antique cast over the entire piece, the cleaning solvent may be applied to a cloth and used to remove as much of the paint residue as needed.

SHELLAC

Sometimes a flat paint needs life added to it or, for some reason, a shinier surface than wax can provide is wanted. A coat of shellac over paint or a wax surface will provide additional gloss and shine.

The shellac can be applied by dipping, brushing, or wiping on with a soft cloth. Dipping gives a heavy, smooth coating, and brushing provides a thinner coating. When applying shellac to wax with a brush, always use a soft brush because a stiff-bristled brush seems to generate bubbles in the paint. Wiping on with a cloth leaves a thin film that does not have the gloss of the other two methods.

3
Sand-Cast Candles

If you want to find out whether you and candle-making are compatible companions without investing any money in molds, you might start with sand-cast candles or rolled beeswax candles. These candles require a minimum amount of materials and are so easy to make that even the first one will be a success.

Wet sand is the mold for the sand-cast candle, and the only other supplies you need are wax, dye, and wick. A container of some sort is necessary to hold the sand, and this can be a large mixing bowl, a foil-lined carboard box, bucket, plastic dishpan, or anything else you may have around the house that is large enough and waterproof enough to make the size candles you want.

There are all sorts of sands, and each one will produce a candle with a slightly different texture from that of another sand. As I am surrounded by desert, most of my candles are made with desert sand which is almost white and has a very fine texture. However, the coarser sands provide a more interesting surface, and I try to vary the textures sometimes with silica sand, builder's sand, or other types.

To make a sand-cast candle fill a container about two-thirds full of sand and then water down the sand. Mix the sand with your hands until every grain of sand is damp. When the sand is wet enough to hold a shape without crumbling, it is ready for shaping into a mold. Your hands, spoons, cups, or any number of objects can be used to scoop out the mold.

Pack the sand well and level it. Then begin digging a hole in the sand and place the removed sand in another container. When a hole the correct size and shape has been formed, pat the sides of the mold hole with your fingers to get rid of the loose sand. On intricate molds it is sometimes helpful to have handy a plastic spray bottle filled with water, in case the sand dries out too fast.

Another way to make the mold is to place a bowl or other object in a hole and pack the sand around it. When the bowl is removed, the sand will retain the shope of the bowl. The only restriction on making a mold in this manner is the shape of the object imbedded in the sand. It can't have a bottom larger than the top, curved sides, or any other irregularities that would prevent easy removal from the sand.

The only other two really important things you need to know about sand cast-candles concern the temperature of the wax and the wetness of the sand. The combination of very hot wax and sand that is just damp enough to hold its shape will produce a candle with a thick sand crust on the outside. In reverse, wax poured at a low temperature into a very wet sand mold will have little or no sand stick to it. If a thick crust of sand and an intricate shape are wanted, work with wet sand until the desired shape is achieved and then let the sand dry before pouring in the hot wax.

In Illustration No. 1, a bowl was used to make the mold for a round candle with a thick sand crust. In the same illustration, the molds for the other two candles were made by using my hands to dig a hole. The feet were added by using my fingers and knuckles to poke holes in the sand.

Objects may be imbedded in the sand candles as shown in Illustration No. 2. Push the objects so that they are partially embedded in the sides of the sand mold. In other words, the decorations should be about half in the sand with the other half sticking out on the inside of the mold. If this is done, you can be sure that the decorations will be securely held by the hot wax.

The candle with the scalloped sides was made by hollowing out a circle in the sand and then taking a small plastic pill bottle and pressing it against the inside of the mold. The glass beads were then pressed into the outside curves of the scallops.

The fluted edges of the candle decorated with seashells were made by digging shallow depressions with a spoon in the sand around the top of the mold.

Everybody likes money, and when it's absolutely impossible to decide on a suitable gift, a money candle might be a solution. Take shiny coins and push the edges into the sand. If you want to put some extra coins in the center, don't fill the mold all the way to the top of the sand. When the wax is firm, push the coins into the wax, keeping them away from the wick. Pour the final layer of wax, and when this wax has cooled somewhat, decorate the top of the candle with a few coins.

Illustration No. 1. *Basic sand-cast candles.*

Illustration No. 2. *Sand-cast candles with imbedded shells and glass beads.*

Illustration No. 3. *Candles with sand/wax shells.*

A different kind of sand candle can be made by making a shell of wax and sand and then filling the shell with wax. Illustration No. 3 shows two examples of candles made this way. When making a candle using this method, the wax and sand are mixed together with approximately three parts of sand to one part of hot wax. These proportions can be varied for different effects.

The low, bowl-shaped candle was made by greasing the outside and bottom of a mixing bowl and applying the wax and sand mixture to the upside-down bowl with a knife. As the wax cools, it can be patted with your hands if a smoother surface is wanted. Any time wax is molded on the outside of an object it should be removed as soon as possible to avoid cracks caused by the contraction of the cooling wax. If there are some cracks, these can be filled in with the sand and wax mixture and will not show. If there is any problem in removing the shell from the mold, fill the container with hot water and the shell will slide off.

When the shell has cooled enough to handle comfortably, more of the sand and wax can be added to form designs. Let the shell cool completely before filling it with wax, and pour the wax at a low temperature to avoid melting the shell.

The Tiki candle was made in a two-piece plaster mold. A spoon was used to line the sides of the mold pieces with the sand and wax. As soon as the wax was cool enough to touch, fingers were used to press it firmly against the mold walls to pick up as much detail as possible. All wax protruding above the top of the mold sections was carefully trimmed away with a knife so that the top of the shell and the mold were flush. This is necessary to insure that the two pieces will fit together snugly.

When the wax was cold, the casting was removed from the mold and the two sides joined together with some of the hot wax/sand mixture. After this had cooled, the shell was filled with wax.

To make a crying Tiki out of this candle, small holes were dug upward under the protruding forehead above the eyes. When the candle had burned down to a certain level, the wax dripped through these holes and down the cheeks. Don't try to cut out the eyes to make these holes because you'll get a stream of wax instead of a trickle. A small hole is all that is necessary.

Should you want a candle with an unusual shape but prefer it without a coating of sand, dig out a sand mold and line it with aluminum foil. If the foil is crumpled before it is placed in the mold, you will have a textured surface rather than a smooth one. If any pieces of the foil become embedded in the wax, they can be removed once the candle is completed by dipping in boiling water until the pieces are melted off. The layered candle in Illustration No. 4 was made by this method.

The other candle in Illustration No. 4 was made in a very wet sand, and random holes were poked with fingers and a pencil. In this case, very wet sand means sand that would ooze water when something was pressed against it.

Driftwood, tree branches, and roots can be incorporated into your sand candles to form legs or a base. Illustration No. 5 shows two examples of using wood for legs and a base. This not only gives the candles something to stand or sit on but adds considerable interest to the candles.

To make this type of candle it is almost necessary to build your mold around the wood. For the candle with the four legs, a square was dug out of the sand, and the sand at the bottom was patted as smooth and flat as possible. The thickness of the sand between the bottom of the container and the bottom of the sand mold should be between one and two inches. There are two reasons for this; one is to have a sufficient amount of sand to hold the legs in place, and the other is so the bottom of the legs can rest on the bottom of the container. If the legs

Illustration No. 4. *Examples of candles cast in wet sand and foil lined sand molds.*

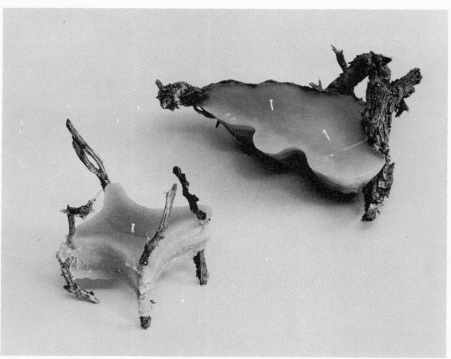

Illustration No. 5. *Sand-cast candles utilizing wood for legs and base.*

are pushed all the way to the bottom of the container, it will assure that they will be level, and there will be no wobble or unevenness when the candle is removed and standing. If this is not done, it may be necessary to trim some of the legs to assure that the candle will be level.

Once the legs were in place, additional sand was patted along the sides of the square hole to make the sides concave. Care was taken to see that the legs were not covered with sand during this part of the mold building. The legs should stand free so that they will be surrounded and held securely by the wax when it is poured.

For the other candle in this illustration a hole was made in the sand large enough for the branch to fit in. Once the branch was in the correct position, a layer of sand was placed along the bottom of the container. The sand mold was then built up around the outside of the branch and the front side of the candle.

Both of these candles were made in very wet sand molds, and nothing was done to them before the picture was taken except hose off the excess sand. As you can see, there is practically no sand sticking to the wax.

Floaters can also be made in sand by digging flat, shallow molds. The small candle in Illustration No. 6 was made with a shallow hole in the sand, and then the handle of an ice pick was pressed into the sand along the outside edges of the mold.

Hanging candles are attractive and popular but they scare me. If they are forgotten and burn down completely, they could very easily set the leather straps on fire. So, if you want to hang a candle, please put it in some sort of fireproof container.

If you like the sand-cast look but don't like the fire hazard, make your container of plaster. Mix water and plaster together as you would for making anything of plaster, and then add sand to this mixture. Make a form in damp sand, and when the plaster mixture is thick enough to scoop up with your hand, line the inside of the mold with it. Another way is to pour the plaster into the mold and then remove the plaster from the center as it hardens.

If these methods don't give you as thick a sand coating as you would like, coat the outside of the shell with glue and roll in dry sand. Tempra paints can be added to the water and plaster mix for color. In fact, the tempras can be added to the water which is used to wet the sand for molds.

Plaque candles are unusual and easy to make. Take a jar, glass bowl, or anything else with a round, flat bottom or a square, flat bottom and press into damp sand. With a pencil or sharp stick draw designs in the wet sand or make them by poking holes in the sand. Make four of these

Illustration No. 6. *Examples of other methods of sand-casting.*

molds and fill them with wax. When the wax is hard, dig a hole in wet sand large enough to hold the four discs, and pack sand around them so they will stand upright. Pour hot wax in the center.

Sand-cast chunk candles are made the same way as any other imbedded sand candle. Pieces of wax are pushed into the sand about halfway, and the center of the mold is filled with hot wax.

A wire-core wick and wick tab can be used in a sand mold before pouring the candle. However, it is much less trouble to insert the wick after the candle is poured.

Sand-cast candles should not be disturbed until the wax is cold. Then dig the sand away from the sides of the candle and lift it out. Scrub under running water with a stiff brush to remove all excess sand. The bottoms should be leveled in the same way as any other candle.

If it is desired to remove all traces of sand from the candle, it can be dipped in boiling water until all the sand has been melted off. The chunk candle in Illustration No. 6 was finished in this manner.

Another way to remove excess sand is with a propane torch. With the torch it is possible to remove all the sand or only portions of it. The flame can be used to remove strips of sand so that there are alternating rows of sand and wax. It can also melt off patches of sand so that even a heavily sand-crusted candle will have wax windows that glow when lighted.

Butterflies seem to be in right now, and some of the sand-cast ones are beauties. Scoop out the sand in the outline of a butterfly and pour wax in different colored layers. A sand wall can be built between the body and the wings and the body poured in black. When the wax is hard, scrape away the sand and pour the wings.

Designs of all shapes and sizes may be made in the wings by building wet sand mounds. When the wings are poured and the candle is taken from the mold, the sand should be pushed from the candle and the sides of the resulting holes scraped. Then place the candle in another bed of sand and fill the holes with different colors.

Another way to make holes for refilling is to press greased glasses, tin cans, and other suitable containers into the bottom of the mold before pouring. Be certain these objects have no undercuts to make removal difficult. When the wax is firm, give the class or can a couple of twists and remove it from the wax. Refill the holes with any combination of colors that harmonize with the main body of wax.

Another attractive sand candle is made by cutting warm wax into thin strips about one inch wide. Start at one end and roll the strip just as you would roll a beeswax candle. Add a strip of another color and continue rolling until the roll of wax is as wide as needed. Several color strips in each roll add to the attractiveness of this candle, but only one color can be used if desired. Make three more rolls in a similar manner and press a roll in each side of a square sand mold. Pour the candle, and when it is removed, either dip in boiling water or remove all sand with a torch. Each side will then have a lovely, multicolored design visible.

Thicker strips can be placed upright around the inside of the sand mold to make a striped candle, and flat designs of all kinds can be cut from wax and pressed against the sides of the mold. If necessary, these designs can be held in place with wax chunks.

It is easy to see from these few examples that much can be accomplished with sand and wax. These candles are not only unusual in appearance, they also appeal to a wide range of tastes. Most candle stores don't consider their stocks complete without at least a few of these on their shelves.

4
Rolled Beeswax Candles

Rolled beeswax candles, like sand-cast candles, do not require molds of any kind. However, they differ in one important respect—the wax is not melted and poured. Beeswax candles could be the answer for those looking for a way to make candles without the usual mess. If wax is dropped on the floor, the cleanup is simple. The pieces are merely picked up off the floor, and unless the wax is stepped on before it is picked up, there is no time spent scraping.

Since no fire is required and therefore no hot wax, this is an ideal project for children. They can't get burned or cut themselves on sharp mold corners, and cleaning up is so easy they can handle it themselves.

Sheets of beeswax can be obtained from any candle-supply house or from your local hobby shop. Some beeswax sheets are smooth and some have a honeycomb pattern. Which you use is a matter of personal preference, but the smooth sheets are usually better for making flowers than the patterned ones.

Scissors or a small knife are necessary for cutting the wax, and a heating pad turned low can be a warmer. Since cold wax has a tendency to crack, it should be warmed to the point where this cracking will not occur. During the summer months the sheets can be placed in the sun for a few minutes until they are plastic enough for working. Holding a sheet several inches above a stove burner for a few seconds will also warm the wax sufficiently.

Because beeswax has a natural adhesive quality, glitter, sequins and small wax decorations will adhere without glue when the two are pressed together.

Eliminating as much air as possible when rolling the candles is the most important aspect of successful rolled candles. The less air that is trapped when rolling, the better the candle burns.

Place the wick at the edge of the sheet and fold over just enough of the sheet to cover the wick. Then press the fold firmly against the wick. Roll and press again. Spread your fingers apart and roll the wax to the end of the sheet, trying to make the roll as tight as possible and keeping the edges straight.

The candle can be made as thick as desired by rolling additional sheets around the core candle. When the candle is completed, seal and level the bottom by pressing it against a hot, smooth surface.

ROLLED TAPER

Anyone who ever made a beeswax candle probably made this as the first one, and it is still one of the most popular. Cut a sheet of beeswax diagonally from corner to corner. Instead of a rectangular sheet of wax you now have two triangles. Place the wick on the long straight edge and roll to the bottom corner of the triangle. The finished candle will have the cut edge of the triangle in a spiral around the candle. This edge can be emphasized by pulling it slightly away from the candle to form a flare. This flare or spiral is often decorated with sequins or glitter, and they may be put on after the candle is finished or pressed into place before the candle is rolled.

To make the rolled tapers in two or more colors, cut a triangle across the wax sheet. Cut additional triangles of complimentary colors and make each triangle slightly smaller than the previous one. Stack the sheets of wax with the smallest on the bottom and roll all of them together.

A straight taper is made by rolling a straight sheet of wax to the desired thickness. If the sheet is rolled evenly, the top of the candle will be flat. If a tapered top is desired, roll the sheet at a slight angle so that each roll is slightly below the previous one. Rolling the candle in this manner will mean that there will be a small amount of excess wax on the bottom of the candle that will have to be trimmed or melted off.

PILLAR CANDLE

The pillar candle is one which is made by rolling as many sheets of wax as necessary to get the desired diameter.

Illustration No. 7. ***Patchwork and rolled beeswax candles.***

Two variations of the straight rolled beeswax candle, or pillar candle, are shown in Illustration No. 7. For the one on the left, the candle was first rolled to the desired thickness, and the top was pressed into a cone shape. Contrasting strips of wax were cut and rolled around the top and bottom. Small strips of beeswax were formed into a roll and placed on the edges of the contrasting strips. Another long, thin strip of the same color was rolled and placed between the two strips in a spiral around the candle. Bits of wax were made into balls and stuck to the candle between the spiral strip.

A spiral design was used on the other candle which consisted of three rolled strips of wax. Two of the strips were the same color and the third a contrasting color. These strips were then wound around the candle with a contrasting color in the middle. Shorter strips of the two colors were rolled and placed between the spirals, alternating the colors.

The large candle is a pillar candle poured in a mold with regular candle wax but covered with torn pieces of beeswax to form a patchwork pattern. The end of a lighted electric light bulb was passed gently over the joining edges of the wax to be certain they would all stick together. The light bulb could also be used with enough pressure and enough heat to melt some of the beeswax so that portions would be smooth to contrast with the honeycomb pattern.

Some very unusual candles could be made by taking old quilt patterns and adapting them to candles. I haven't seen any quilting patterns for years, but I'm sure there are some around. With the current rage for nostalgia, they might make quite a splash. The beeswax sheets could be stacked so that several patterns could be cut at one time, and then the pieces of the pattern assembled and pressed onto a beeswax candle.

In case any of you are wondering about the wick on the patchwork candle, it's too long. Somehow I failed to trim it and didn't notice the error until I saw the photograph. So, this one can be used as an example of what not to do.

TWISTED TAPERS

The tall taper in Illustration No. 8 is a folded, rather than a rolled, candle. Decide how wide you want the candle and place the wick in the center of the first fold. Continue folding the sheet until it is as thick as needed. After each fold press lightly along the length of the fold with the heel of your hand to eliminate as much air as possible. The candle can be made in two colors by cutting a strip of wax slightly smaller than the folds and pressing it onto one side of the candle. If the wax is cold, warm it slightly and then gently twist the candle into the desired shape.

CHRISTMAS TREE

The Christmas tree began with a sheet of wax rolled into a pillar candle and the top molded to a point. A paper pattern was made for the branches so that they would be uniform in size. One side of the pattern was cut straight to fit against the candle, and the other side had jagged edges to represent tree branches. Four sheets of wax were stacked and six sheets of branches cut from the sheets, using the paper pattern. The branches were placed around the candle and fastened by running a hot ice pick along both sides of the branch where it joined the candle. The branches were too heavy to simply press against the candle to make them stick. When all the branches were in place and fastened securely, the tree was sprinkled heavily with glitter, and a small beeswax roll was placed around the bottom.

Illustration No. 8. *Novelty beeswax candles.*

SCULPTURED BEESWAX

These are a little harder and more time-consuming than the plain rolled beeswax candles, but they are also a lot more fun. The mushroom candle is probably the easiest, and I'll start with that one.

Rolled Beeswax Candles

Stack six sheets of beeswax and cut a circle. Pull and press the beeswax circles until a half-ball effect is achieved. Roll a short candle with a long wick and then punch a hole through the mushroom top. Thread the wick through this hole and weld the stem and the mushroom top together with a hot ice pick. Tear off small pieces of wax and press them to the top of the mushroom. Place a beeswax roll of the same color around the stem of the mushroom.

This can't be seen in the picture, but ribs, or whatever they are called, were placed on the underside of the mushroom. To make the ribs, place tiny, rolled strips underneath the mushroom, radiating out from the stem like spokes on a wagon wheel. These ribs can be made more visible by tilting the mushroom cap when it is attached to the stem.

ROSE

The rose can double as a candle to sit on a shelf or table or be put in a bowl of water as a floater. Roses can be made as large or small as wanted, and very large ones can be utilized as swimming pool floaters for a festive party. Also, I once heard of a hostess who filled her bathtub with colored water and floated lighted, scented candles in the tub during a party. However, most floaters are found drifting in brandy snifters, punch bowls, or large glass dishes.

To make the rose, cut a circle of green beeswax and then cut leaves and press all around the circle. Cut oval or egg-shaped petals and place them on top of the leaves, pressing each one firmly in place. Add petals until the rose is as thick as wanted but keep the petals to the outside, away from the center. For the center, roll a short candle and shape it with your fingers at the top so that it comes to a point. Also, shape the bottom slightly so that it is not completely flat. Cut a rectangular strip of wax and spiral it around the candle, fluting the edges. Place this in the center of the petals and shape the petals around it.

OWL

The owl begins as a straight rolled candle, and wax is added to this core or base to give it shape. Cut strips of wax and roll them around the candle. Make the thickest rolls in the middle of the body and the middle of the head. Cut more strips in graduated sizes and thicknesses and roll them around the body so that the wax tapers at

41

the neck and feet. Treat the head in the same way, with most of the thickness in the middle of the face. If necessary, fill in the areas between the strips with pieces of wax so that the owl is fairly smooth. The wax can also be pressed and kneaded with your fingers to help obtain the contours you want. When the head and body are approximately the right size and shape, cut large pieces of wax and cover the entire figure with wax pieces. This insures a more finished look in the places where there are no feathers or where the wax shows through the feathers.

To make the wings, roll two strips of wax and taper the ends so that most of the fullness is in the center. Place these rolls along the sides of the body, using a hot ice pick, if necessary, to make them stay in place.

The feet were made of several flattened balls of wax, and then the feathers were applied. To make the feathers, cut small oval pieces of beeswax. This goes faster if several thicknesses are cut at one time. Beginning at the bottom of the owl, press the feathers to the body so that they overlap. Fill in with these feathers all the way to the neck. Cut feathers of a constrasting color and apply them to the wings in the same manner.

Next put feathers around the lower portion of the front of the head and use them to cover the back of the head. Make a hooked, pointed bill and put it in the center of the face. Roll a strip of beeswax, bend it in the middle to form a V-shape, and place the center of it on top of the bill. Bring the ends of the strip to the outer top of the head to form the ears.

Cut two sets of circles for the eyes, one slightly larger than the other. Place the small circle on the larger circle and press into place with the handle of an X-Acto knife. Make the pressure hard enough so that there are two holes in the centers of the circles. Fill these holes with two balls of beeswax and you have a reasonable facsimile of an owl.

These examples are a small sample of the many ways beeswax sheets can be converted to candles, but they will give you an idea of the possibilities.

5
Year-Round Candles

A few short years ago, the only occasion on which a candle was in evidence around the house, except for tapers on the dinner table now and then, was at Christmas. These Christmas candles were displayed for two or three weeks and then banished to a corner shelf for the rest of the year. Things have certainly changed since then, and in many homes a candle is as much a part of today's decor as a vase or an ashtray.

Although people still buy more Christmas candles than any other kind and possibly will always do so, the candle that can be used as a decorative accent all year is coming into its own. There are many individuals who love candles and want to be surrounded by them. Others often find that only a candle is exactly right for some particular spot in a room. Whatever the reason, the candle that can serve as a decoration, as a conversation piece, or even as a space filler is being sought out more and more. After all, a candle that can be admired fifty-two weeks a year is more practical than one which has a life span of several weeks.

On the following pages you will find candles to fill almost any decorating need. They may be copied, altered, or used as the basis for a candle that is completely different.

WAX APPLIQUÉS

A really elegant candle can be made in a hurry by using wax appliqués. All that is necessary is to find a suitable mold, pour wax into it, and attach the wax decoration to a candle. There are so many good

Illustration No. 9. *Wax appliqués.*

half-molds available now that it's not a matter of having to search for the right mold but of deciding which one to choose. Some of the new mold materials allow for production of molds that capture all the design detail of the original model.

At one time most of the half-molds were fairly large so that the castings could be used for wall plaques but now there are many that are a perfect size for candles. The round and square medallions are especially good with candles, and there are also flowers, animals, figures, and storybook scenes for children.

Some of the newer mold materials do not need to be treated before pouring wax into them. However, to be on the safe side, unless the directions state otherwise, a light coating of oil will be helpful in releasing the casting.

The harlequin figures were poured in plastic half-molds and were painted for picture-taking so that the detail would stand out, but they are more effective if they are left unpainted. Dark figures against a light candle are particularly striking.

To make an appliqué, pour in soft wax and remove the casting as soon as possible so that it may be shaped to the candle before it hardens. Put a light coat of rubber cement on the back of the figure and press gently on the candle. Without applying enough pressure to distort the appliqué, try to press all the edges tight against the candle. The object is to make the decoration appear as part of the candle rather than something that was applied later.

If appliqués harden before they are in place, they may be warmed by putting them under a heating pad or by directing a flow of hot air from a hair dryer on them. By using an electric needle and a feather touch, the edges can be sealed to the candle. Another sealing method is to carefully brush hot wax the same color as the candle around the edges. Use the smallest brush possible for a neat job. (Illustration No. 9.)

QUAIL

The contemporary quail in Illustration No. 10 make attractive candles just as they come from the mold, but they are also perfect for many decorating techniques. Their appearance can be changed by giving them beaded tails and crests.

To make the crest, use regular straight pins and place three small beads on each pin. The pins can be lined up across the top of the head, in a line from front to back, or even placed in a circle. Longer pins, such as corsage pins or hat pins, can be used to make the tails.

Wire can be substituted for the pins, and after the beads are strung on the wire, it can be twisted or curved for an entirely different effect. The wire can be bent in the center and both ends inserted in the wax. If only one end of the wire is pushed into the wax, bend the wire at the other end to keep the beads from slipping off.

Illustration No. 10. *Quail and beads.*

The lack of detail on this or any other plain candle makes an ideal surface for painting or carving. Mexican designs in bright colors would be particularly good on these quail.

ORIENTAL PRINCESS

The Oriental Princess candle is made from a plastic mold and is used to show how a candle arrangement can be made without using flowers.

Pour the princess in flesh-colored wax and then paint the features, hair, and robe. Pour a rectangular base and also a dragon. Attach the candle and dragon to the base and place a gold foil strip around the outside of the base. The partially opened fan may be fastened to the back with pins, or a support may be used behind the fan to hold it upright. (Illustration No. 11.)

Features are difficult for some to paint, so here are a few tips which might help. With many types of paint you can put a dot or two of red paint on the cheeks and then blend with your finger for a slight blush. If the paint you are using won't give you this blush, stay away from bright, garish splotches of color on the cheeks. Only clowns look better with bright red cheeks. No color at all is better than too much.

Illustration No. 11. *Princess and fan.*

When painting eyes and eyebrows, put small dots of paint on the inside and outside corners and join the dots with lines of paint. These dots make it easier to get the eyes and brows the same size on each side of the face. It also eliminates the problem of getting one eye lower than the other or one eyebrow higher than the other. Don't join the corners of the eyelids when painting them but leave a small open space at each corner. To avoid a startled look, have little or no white showing beneath the dark portion of the eyeball and lower lid.

Rather than paint in a solid mass of color on the mouth, leave a very thin line between the upper and lower lips. Also use a pink of some shade for the lips rather than a bright red.

These are very simple rules, but if they are followed, they will aid a great deal in painting on an attractive, symmetrical face rather than a lopsided one.

RICE PAPER/TISSUE PAPER

The beauty of rice paper for candles is that when wet it is practically transparent. When sodium silicate is brushed on or when the paper is dipped in wax, the same transparenty is achieved. This paper is thin enough so that it is possible to place it over almost any pattern or design and trace whatever you want. In Illustration No. 12, the peacock was traced from a design book. Do your tracing lightly, no heavy black lines. Also, cut the paper to the exact size of the candle before tracing so that the design will be properly positioned. The traced lines may be outlined in gold, as was done on this candle, and then filled in with paint, or the outline can be done last. Practically any paints can be used, even water colors.

When paint is totally dry, wrap paper around candle and fasten. Paper can be attached to the candle with pins, but be sure pinheads are covered. A better way is to use one of the dry spray glues, of which Presto-Stik is among the best. This glue won't wet the paper and won't be visible through it. When the paper is securely fastened to candle, dip the candle in hot wax. The hot wax dip will bring out the transparency of the paper, and it will look as though you painted your design directly on the candle.

Any type of design can be incorporated into a candle by using this technique. No artistic ability is required. All that is necessary is to trace something someone else has done. You can also use this idea as a background for some of your wax decorations since it isn't necessary to cover the entire candle with paper. If the designs are small, they may be cut out and scattered over the candle.

Illustration No. 12. *Rice paper candle.*

The tissue paper candle was covered previously, but there has been a new development since then. The tissue paper candle is made by gluing small, torn pieces of different-colored tissue paper onto a candle. The colors should overlap to some extent so that there is a blending of colors. For example, by starting with red tissue paper pieces at the bottom of a candle and adding yellow and blue, the completed candle will have the colors of red, orange, yellow, green, and blue on it.

There are now on the market tissue papers which bleed when water is applied to them. This opens up a whole new decorating area, and it is possible to get some of the most vibrant, splashy colors imaginable when combining these tissues.

One method of applying these tissues is to glue them on the candle just as you do the regular tissue paper. Have the darker colors on the bottom and glue lighter colors over them. If the dark colors are on top, the light colors are drowned by the darker bleeding. Unusual effects can be obtained by pushing and crinkling the tissue as it is glued to the candle rather than trying for a smooth surface. When the candle has been covered with tissue paper, dip fingers, sponge, or brush in water and wet the paper. To begin with, don't cover the entire candle with water; leave some of the areas dry. Wherever the water touches the tissue, the colors burst in all directions. Dip the candle when the paper has dried.

An even more spectacular blending of colors can be achieved by covering a piece of rice paper the size of a candle with pieces of tissue and then wetting. When dry, remove the tissue and you will find that the dye has been transferred to the rice paper. As a bonus, it's not only possible to cover a candle with the rice paper, but another candle can be decorated with the tissue paper used to color the rice paper. There is still enough color left in the tissue so that it can be used and nothing is wasted.

No matter which method is used, each candle will be an original since it would be impossible to make two alike.

Neither the tissue paper nor the rice paper should be used with small candles. Either place the paper around the bottom of a candle or decorate only the larger-diameter candles so there will be no chance of the candle flame coming in contact with the decoration. Incidentally, this type of decoration is particularly appropriate for hurricane candles because the light will shine through the colors.

If these bleeding tissue papers are not available locally, you may write to the Austen Display, Inc., 133 West 19th St., New York, N.Y. 10011. They will be able to tell you of any dealers in your area, or you may order from them direct. The tissues come in 42 different colors so there should be something to please everyone.

HURRICANE CANDLES

Building up a large stock of molds is a rather expensive project, but as shown previously, it is possible to make candles without investing in molds. Making hurricane candles from slabs of wax is another way to do this.

If possible, use a large pan for pouring your wax so that all the pieces can be cut from the same sheet and will be of equal thicknesses. Grease the pan and pour wax to the desired depth. Cut a paper pattern so that all the sides will be uniform. Place this pattern over the wax and cut four sides before the wax becomes hard. A bottom may also be cut at the same time, but it is not essential if the finished hurricane is placed on a stand of some sort.

Remove the sides from the pan and fasten the corners together with hot wax or by using an electric needle or soldering gun. Level the bottom and top on a hot surface. The corners will fit better and have a neater appearance if they are beveled. Also, a hot wax dip will usually improve the looks of these hurricanes.

If you want more than just a plain candle, there are all kinds of ways it can be decorated. If you can paint, you have four smooth, flat surfaces on which to display your talent. Another method is to carve or incise designs. This is quite effective because of the contrast between the high and low points when the candle is burning. A candle poured in two colors and carved down to the second color offers even more contrast.

Don't assemble the candle until the carving is completed. It is much easier to carve on the flat slabs than trying to decide where to hold the candle after it's all put together. Linoleum carving tools make shorter work of gouging out the wax but small, sharp knives also do a good job.

When carving, there is less chance of chipping the surrounding wax if the first cutting or carving is shallow. Once a track is made for the design, it can be made as deep or as shallow as wanted.

If you have a very steady hand, a light touch, and a small hobby drill, you can get some interesting textures in your carvings by lightly going over the carved areas with some of the attachments, such as brushes or burrs. Be very careful to barely touch the surface of the carving. If pressure is applied, the drill will cut all the way through the shell.

WINDOW HURRICANE

The shell of a hurricane candle is made by removing the film of wax at the top of the candle after it has reached a thickness of about one-fourth of an inch. The liquid wax is then poured out of the center of the candle, leaving it hollow.

To make the window hurricane candle in Illustration No. 13, either cut holes in the side of candle while the wax is still warm, but the candle is still in the mold or cut the holes after the candle has been removed. It's easier to cut the holes while the candle is in the mold and

Illustration No. 13. *Window hurricane.*

then push out the cut wax when the candle is removed. Cookie cutters are great for cutting holes in warm wax.

After the candle is removed, trim the holes with a knife. Cut pieces of rice paper or some other transparent paper slightly larger than the holes and glue to the inside of the candle so that the holes are covered. When the glue is dry, lay candle flat and spray the paper on the outside with glitter cement or cover it with a transparent glue. Sprinkle on small, glass-reflective beads which are available at wholesale florists. Tiny pieces of crushed glass from the hobby shop may also be used.

The openings can be outlined with jewels, gold braid, whipped wax, and so on. In the candle shown, gold foil medallions with an open design were placed over the openings so that they also covered the cut edges.

A variation of this idea is to cover the holes with heavy lace which has been dipped in hot wax. Lace edging can be used to disguise the edges of the holes. For a very delicate, feminine candle cover the edges of the holes with whipped wax and insert small flowers and leaves.

CHINESE HURRICANE

If making round or square hurricane candles is becoming a bore, alter the appearance of a square hurricane candle by adding a new side. While the shell is still in the mold but before the wax has hardened, cut along the corners and bottom of one side. When the shell is removed from the mold, carefully push out the cut side.

A new side must be poured to replace the old one and the first step is to pour wax into an oiled pan to the desired thickness. Next cut a paper pattern in any shape you like so long as it is large enough to cover the open side. Place the pattern on the warm wax and cut out the side.

Imbedding is another possibility if it is possible to find small, flat objects that aren't too thick. Pretty buttons, flowers, and half-round plastic figures are a few of the things that could be used. Lightly glue the decorations facedown in the pan and then pour the wax over them.

There are many plastic molds that are approximately the size of a square hurricane, and a side can be poured in one of these molds. If a mold the exact size can't be located, use one slightly larger. Often the candle is more unique if the side extends a little beyond the candle.

The front side of the hurricane candle in Illustration No. 14 was poured in a plastic mold, painted, and then attached to the candle. Hot wax or a soldering gun will hold it together.

COOKING CRYSTALS

Still another idea for making a different hurricane is to buy some cooking crystals from the hobby shop and make different-colored stones. The container for cooking these crystals in the kitchen oven can be pieces of aluminum foil with the edges turned up to form a bowl shape.

Cover the hurricane shell thickly with whipped wax or Whip Wax

Illustration No. 14. *Chinese hurricane.*

and press the stones into the wax. Since the shell is covered with whipped wax, it can be poured more thinly that usual so that the light will shine through the stones. For even more light, cut holes in the shell smaller than the stones and place the stones over the holes. (Illustration No. 15.)

FLOWER POTS

Plastic flowerpots make great molds, and candles can be poured and burned in the clay pots. The clay pots are ideal containers for citronella candles that are burned outdoors to keep the bugs away. The addition of a few simple designs in bright-colored paints will change them from utility candles to decorator items.

To make the candles in Illustration No. 16, small plastic pots were used for the molds. On one of the candles, the rim and bottom were

Illustration No. 15. *Hurricane decorated with cooking crystals.*

Illustration No. 16. *Small flowerpot candles.*

trimmed with wax flowers from a press mold, and on the other, ruffles were the decoration. Wax ruffles are made by fluting strips of soft wax with your fingers and attaching them to the candle with hot wax or an electric needle. Small wax-dipped flowers were placed between the two rows of ruffles at the top of the pot.

Scented flowerpot candles are a lovely gift for a sick friend. They can be dressed up by adding flowers to the outside of the pot, covering with heavy lace, texturing, or adding foil medallions. It would be impossible to obtain a plaster or plastic candle mold for the price of a flower pot, so they really do have a lot going for them.

A large pot was the mold for the candle in Illustration No. 17. The wick was left long, and a mound of whipped wax built up on the top of the pot. This wax mound was then covered thickly with wax roses and leaves.

Be sure to oil the inside of the pot or spray with a good release spray before pouring. It might be a good idea to buy the smallest pots you can find for experimenting. Because of the differences in plastics, it is not possible to give a specific temperature for pouring. Some plastics can

Illustration No. 17. *Flowerpot candle with roses.*

tolerate much less heat than others, and wax poured too hot will cause a collapsed mold and spilled wax. However, the higher the temperature of the wax (within a reasonable range), the better the surface of the candle. This is the purpose of the small experimental molds—to try different temperatures of wax to determine how much heat the larger plastic pots can stand without melting.

57

Illustration No. 18. *Sea life candle.*

If there are holes in the bottom of the pot, plug them with clay or sealer before pouring.

SEA LIFE

Candles decorated with sea life seem to me to be particularly appropriate for bathrooms. This is not as farfetched as it might sound since more and more people are decorating their bathrooms as carefully as they do the rest of the house. Candles in the bathroom are not only decorative, but a burning candle does double duty by eliminating bathroom odors.

A candle with a base provides more decorating area when using seashells. In Illustration No. 18, the base was covered with fairly large

Illustration No. 19. *Candle decorated with mermaid.*

shells. Smaller shells were added to the sides of the candle with the smallest shells near the top. The shells and other sea life can be attached to the candle with adhesive, and by dipping the base of the candle in hot wax, the large shells will be cemented in place.

In Illustration No. 19, a mermaid from a plastic mold has a prominent spot on a background of sea fans and starfish. A row of small shells circles the bottom of the candle, and plastic bubbles float to the top of the candle.

FLOWERS

It is doubtful that anything will ever replace flowers as the favorite candle decoration. On the following pages you will find many ways in which they can be used.

Decorating with plastic flowers is one of the fastest and easiest ways to make a stunning candle out of a plain one. It seems the plastic flowers get more lifelike all the time, and the colors and types are almost unlimited. There are even some that Mother Nature never thought of making.

A lovely fall candle might be decorated with the oranges, reds, yellows, and greens of autumn. For the candle in Illustration No. 20, a background of oak leaves was pinned to the sides of the candle, and a red and orange plastic shrimp plant fastened on top of the leaves and curved slightly to one side. The chrysanthemums were arranged in a curve down the side and base of the candle, and the pheasant added after all the other decorations were in place. The pheasant was poured in wax and painted, but any kind of animal or figure would be appropriate.

TIGER LILY

Beginning candle decorators tend to be a bit hesitant about putting large, splashy flowers on a candle. There is a feeling that the candle will be overpowered by the decoration and that small flowers would be safer. However, if large flowers or other types of decorations are placed to the side of the candle, there is an impression of openness, and the candle is still plainly visible.

The tiger lily candle in Illustration No. 21 is an example of this type of decorating. Cut a sea fan in half and place in the center front of candle. Pin plastic tiger lilies and buds down the sides and to the front bottom of the candle. Shells, bits of coral, and starfish were fastened

Illustration No. 20. *Fall candle with pheasant.*

to the base of the candle along with a wax "tiger" fish. Small starfish can be fastened to the sea fan with adhesive. Because of the holes in the sea fan and the slender petals of the lilies, these decorations don't appear to be as heavy as they actually are.

Another example of this type of decorating in Illustration No. 22

Illustration No. 21. *Tiger lily candle.*

shows some rather solid decorations which would be too heavy if they covered the front of the candle.

The canna leaves were cut from wax sheets to the desired size and veined with a paintbrush handle. This arrangement uses six large leaves in graduated sizes, two leaf tips in front and three on the opposite side of the iris. After all the leaves are cut, they were warmed so that they were pliable enough to bend until the two sides were almost touching. At the bottom of the leaf, the two sides were pressed together firmly to eliminate bulk. The leaves were fastened to the candle in a half circle, beginning with the largest leaf at the top. Three long, slender plastic leaves were pinned to the candle next to the largest canna leaf and then twisted and curved downward. It was necessary to pin the tips of these

Illustration No. 22. *Iris and canna leaves.*

Illustration No. 23. *Carnation-decorated candle.*

leaves to the candle to hold them in place. The iris was curved down the front of the candle, being careful that the ends of the canna leaves were covered by the overlapping flowers. In addition to being part of the decoration, the leaf tips were placed so they covered any stem ends.

CARNATIONS

Variety is as desirable in candlemaking as it is in any other en-

Candles showing a variety of decorating techniques.

Christmas candles showing different ways of decorating with bells.

deavor. For a change of pace, the candle in Illustration No. 23 utilizes small flowers for a less ornate appearance.

Plastic scotch broom was pinned to the candle so that it formed a half circle. It was necessary to use several sprays of varying lengths to achieve the desired shape. The paper flowers were dipped in wax several times so that they looked more like wax flowers than paper. Three buds were pinned to the candle, following the upper curve of the broom. The plastic leaves were attached next and then the carnations.

Several hours spent studying flower arranging books from the local library will reward you with many ideas for making flower-decorated candles. It will be time well spent.

IMBEDDED FLOWERS

If you prefer your decorations inside the candle, that's easily arranged also. Floral Fantasy is the name of this unusual type of candle, and it is striking. Any plastic flower can be used, but the most successful candles are made with flowers which are fairly flat. Daisies, pansies, poinsettias, wild roses, dogwood, and apple blossoms are some of the flowers which are most appropriate.

The flowers are arranged on a core candle and then inserted into a mold. You may use any method you like for attaching the flowers to the core candle. Small pins do a good job and so does hot wax. The hot wax can be used only if the core candle and flowers form a tight fit inside the mold. Otherwise, the wax holding the flowers to the core would melt when the candle is poured, and the flowers would slip out of place.

The wick of the core candle must be threaded through the wick hole in the mold. The best way I have found for doing this is to thread very thin wire through the wick hole in the bottom of the mold and pull it to the top of the mold. Wrap the wire as tightly as possible around the wick of the core candle several times and brush over the wire and wick with hot wax. When the wax is cold, slip the decorated core candle gently into the mold. As the core candle is lowered into the mold, very carefully draw the wire back through the wick hole until the wick has been pulled through. If you tug too hard, the wire will slip off the wick. The object is to guide the wick through the hole rather than trying to pull it through. Secure the wick as you would for pouring any candle.

If you pour your core candle, leave a long wick on both ends. A long wick at the top helps when threading it through the wick hole. A

Illustration No. 24. *Floral fantasy candles.*

long wick on the bottom can be attached to a wick rod at the top of the mold so that the core does not rest on the bottom of the mold but is raised at least one-half inch.

If the wick on a core candle has already been trimmed, it can be threaded through the hole, but it takes a little more patience. A longer wick can be made by cutting off the existing wick even with the top of the candle and inserting another wick. To do this, melt a hole about half an inch deep against the candle wick with a hot ice pick and insert another wick in this hole. The same thing can be done on the bottom of the candle. If the two wicks are placed side by side, as the new wick burns down, it will ignite the wick already in the candle.

It is also possible to insert a plain core candle in the mold and push the flowers down around it. There will be less control over the placement of the flowers, but it can be done this way.

Another method is to partially fill the mold with wax chunks. Then put the flowers in the mold and hold them against the sides of the mold. Pack wax chunks in the center of the mold between the flowers to hold the flowers in place.

Always keep in mind that the bottom of the mold will be the top of the candle and plan your decorating accordingly.

When the core candle in in place, pour in clear, hot wax just as you would for any other candle. If the core candle is poured in a color, enough of the wax will melt so that the finished candle will be a softer version of that color.

Pansies, leaves, and tiny flower clusters were used in make the candle in Illustration No. 24. This candle is shown in color on the book jacket.

The daisy and butterfly candle in Illustration No. 24 was made exactly the same as the pansy candle. However, one more step was added after the candle was removed from the mold. Water was heated in a roasting pan, and the candle was rolled in boiling water to melt off a portion of the wax. As the wax melted, parts of the decorations were released from the wax. The finished candle has some of the decorations still embedded in the wax and some on the outside of the candle.

DRIFTWOOD

Sculpturing wax and plastic flowers mix well as shown by Illustration No. 25. The driftwood is made of sculpturing wax, and it is simply a matter of pulling, pinching, and twisting until you get the shape you want. In fact, it's rather hard not to wind up with something that looks like a piece of weathered wood if the wax is the right color. A few holes can be cut or punched in the wax for an even more beat-up look, and a coating of antiquing paint will provide the finishing touch.

Once the driftwood piece is formed, the flowers and leaves can be stuck in the wax while it is still warm, and then the whole thing can be attached to the candle.

This is a versatile candle, and by changing the flowers, it can be

Illustration No. 25. *Daisies and wax driftwood.*

used for any season. It becomes a Christmas candle if holly and poinsettias are used, and by switching to lilies, it becomes an Easter candle. An eye-catching arrangement composed of a black candle, very pale grey driftwood and red flowers will draw "ohs" and "ahs."

BIRD AND DOGWOOD

In Illustration No. 26, all of the wax decorations are from a plaster

Illustration No. 26. *All wax decorations.*

mold. The branches, flowers, and leaves were poured in sculpturing wax and removed from the mold while still pliable. The branch was poured three times, and the pieces were joined together to make a longer branch. While the wax was still warm, it was bent to the shape of the candle, and the flowers and leaves were twisted into more natural positions.

Candle Decorating

I still think the star candle is the hardest to decorate, and unless decorations can be found that are small enough to fit between the points, the only way to handle it is to pretend it's just another round candle. That's the way this one was treated, and the decorations were fastened to the points and the space in between ignored.

MOLDED WAX ROSES

If a poll were taken to determine the world's favorite flower, the rose would probably win by a wide margin. Wax roses made by hand, petal by petal, are more delicate and lifelike than roses made in a mold, but they are also much more time consuming.

By far the best rose mold I have ever found is the one made by Duncan Ceramics in their Student Mold series. There are two rose molds, one of which makes one large rose and a bud, and the other makes two smaller roses. There is also a mold for convincingly natural rose leaves. This mold has leaves in several sizes and also includes a stem with thorns on it. The reason this mold is being given so much space here is because I think it is a mold that should be on every candlemaker's shelf. You will find candles made with this mold throughout the book, and it would put a crimp in my candle decorating if I didn't have it.

The mold comes in three sections, two sections of petals, and a center. When removing the sections from the mold, if a hole is cut in the bottom of the second section, the three pieces can be assembled in one operation. Scoop the largest petal section in hot wax and leave about one-fourth of an inch of wax in the bottom. Put the section with the hole in the bottom inside the larger petals and then place the rose center in the second section of petals. The hot wax in the bottom row of petals will rise through the hole in the second row of petals and hold the rose center in place. This eliminates the necessity of fastening the three pieces together separately.

The roses can be used as they are, but they are improved by a wax dip. Hold the rose by one side and dip it halfway into the hot wax. When the wax cools, dip the other side.

ROSE TOPIARY TREE

The topiary tree makes a very elegant and impressive candle. It is quite large because the dowel stem adds six to eight inches to its height. Poured in white, it can be a special wedding candle, or, poured in color, it makes a lively gift or a distinctive decoration for your own home. It is also quite a conversation piece. The opening remark is usually "That can't be a candle."

Pour a ball candle either in a bowl or a ball mold and make a wax flowerpot from a plastic flowerpot mold. Cut a wooden dowel to the desired length, allowing at least an inch and a half on each end to be inserted in the wax. Wrap satin or velvet ribbon tightly around the dowel and glue the ribbon at each end.

Drill or cut a hole about an inch and a half deep in the bottom of the ball and fill the hole about one-fourth full of very hot wax. Insert one end of the dowel in this hole, making sure that it is straight, and then leave it alone until the wax is absolutely cold. If necessary, add more hot wax so that the hole will be filled level with the bottom of the candle.

When all the wax around the dowel has hardened, you are ready to begin decorating. You will need a fairly large collection of buds, roses, and leaves. These should be poured before you begin assembling the candle.

I find it easier to do the first part of the decorating by holding the ball in my lap. Whether your working surface is your lap or a table, crumple up an old sheet or towel and let the candle rest on that. The reason for this is that a cushion is provided for the flowers as the candle is turned. Start at the bottom of the candle around the dowel stick and cover a portion of the candle with whipped wax. Through trial and error I have found that the best colors for the whipped wax are either green or the color of the roses. If one of these colors is used when there is an open space between the decorations, there will be nothing to distract the eye.

Insert the roses in the whipped wax, keeping them as close together as possible. Have a supply of warm, pliable leaves nearby and use these leaves to fill in the spaces between the flowers. If the leaves can be bent and twisted with ease, it makes it much easier to cover the spaces between the roses. The buds are also used for the purpose of filling in open spaces. When the candle is completed, it should appear to be a mass of roses and leaves with very little whipped wax visible.

When the bottom half of the candle has been decorated, place it on its top and leave it until all the wax is hard. Then turn it right side up and complete the decorating. Try to position the flowers so that there is a rose at the center top of the candle. Make a hole through the center of a rose, thread the wick through the hole and press the rose down into the whipped wax. If there isn't enough space for a rose at the top of the candle, fill in around the wick with leaves and buds.

Don't try to complete the entire candle in one sitting. This is a heavy candle, and its weight will flatten the soft wax if all sides are decorated at one time. Instead of a symmetrical ball, you will have a lopsided mon-

Illustration No. 27. *Rose topiary tree.*

strosity. If you must keep going, work on two candles so that one will have a chance to harden while you are putting roses on the other.

There will be a lot of wax drips from pushing the roses into the whipped wax, and the time to remove them is while decorating, rather than waiting till the candle is finished. If the runs and drips are removed before they harden, they won't have a chance to stick.

Drill a hold about an inch and a half deep in the flower pot, fill the hole with hot wax, and insert the dowel. If wax overflows, it is unimportant because it will be covered later with whipped wax. After the wax has hardened around the dowel, cover the top of the pot with whipped wax and place a few flowers and leaves in the wax. (Illustration No. 27.)

Dipping each rose separately can be a chore, and so, if desired, the ball can be dipped after all the decorations are attached. This not only eliminates dipping each rose but also fastens all the decorations so securely that there is no way they can come off. If it is decided to dip, do this before putting the dowel into the flower pot. The dowel stick makes a perfect handle when dipping the ball into the hot wax.

GRAPE AND ROSE BALL

In Illustration No. 28, the ball and the base or holder are both made of wax to form one large candle. The cherub base is from a mold for a bowl, but it works beautifully as a holder for the candle.

The ball can be used alone without the holder, and it will still be an attractive candle. However, if a base is to be used, wick the mold and pour it in a pastel shade that will compliment the decorated ball.

Cover the ball, using the same method as for the topiary tree. For a candle with such an elaborate, ornate appearance, it is surprisingly easy to make. The two large grape clusters cover almost half of the ball (one on each side), and only the spaces in between have to be filled in with roses and smaller grapes. Rose and grape leaves may be used to cover any open areas.

After the ball is decorated and the base removed from the mold, fill the bowl on top of the base almost half-full of hot wax. Lower gently the candle into the bowl, and when the wax has cooled slightly, fill in around the edge of the bowl with grape leaves.

When the ball has burned down, it may be necessary to dig a little to find the wick in the bowl, but it can then be lighted and the candle burned all the way to the base.

Illustration No. 28. *Grape and rose ball.*

GRAPE CLUSTER

Grapes, whether wax or plastic, are always in demand as candle decorations. Two sections of wax from a fluted salad mold comprise the basic candle in Illustration No. 29. Instead of covering the entire candle, only the top two-thirds was decorated. The eye appeal of this candle will be enhanced if the leaves are poured in varying shades of green. The grapes should also be different shades of the same color; in this case, the color range went from light to dark pink. The candle will have more life if the decorations are composed of more than two colors.

The grapes and leaves were attached with whipped wax, and tendrils made of soft rolled wax were placed near the tops of some of the grapes.

Illustration No. 29. *Grape cluster.*

Illustration No. 30. *Grapes and beads.*

Warm the grapes until they are pliable enough to be bent to fit the curve of the candle. The leaves should also be warmed for ease of handling.

GRAPES AND BEADS

So far, all of the roses and grapes seem to have wound up on ball candles. However, they are just as decorative on a pillar candle as can be seen in Illustration No. 30.

The grape clusters and leaves were put on with whipped wax, and the beads were then twisted around them. If the ends of the beads are buried in the whipped wax, there is no need to tie knots in the string to keep the beads from slipping off. Touches of hot wax can be used to hold the beads against the decorations.

FRAMED ROSES

Wax doesn't necessarily have to be confined to candlemaking but can become part of unusual and one-of-a-kind wall decorations. In Illustration No. 31, velvet-backed wax roses combine with plastic ferns to make a wall hanging that can't be found in any store.

Select a frame and remove the glass. Cut about one-fourth of an inch off the cardboard backing of the frame and cut a piece of velvet about one-half of an inch larger that the cardboard. Glue the edges of the velvet to the back of the cardboard backing, pulling it tight so there are no wrinkles.

Prior to beginning the arrangement, pour as many roses and leaves as will be needed. Before putting the roses together, punch two small holes in the bottom set of petals and insert a piece of small copper wire or carpet thread through the holes. In other words, start on the underside of the petal section, thread the wire through one hole and, then thread it down through the other one so that the ends of the wire are sticking out of the bottom of the petals. Pull the wire through the holes until the ends are approximately the same length. Assemble the roses and dip.

Next, place the frame over the backing and arrange the roses on the velvet until the desired design is obtained. Once everything is arranged to your satisfaction, remove the materials from the velvet and place them on the table, following the same design pattern. Brush the velvet to remove any bits of wax. Crumpled nylon net is excellent for cleaning velvet.

Take the first rose from your design on the table and transfer it to the same position on the velvet. Punch two small holes through the velvet and cardboard and insert a pin or toothpick in each hole. It is almost impossible to find a small hole in velvet, and the toothpicks will keep the holes from getting lost. Push the wires on the bottom of the rose through the holes in the velvet. and fasten them together on the back of the cardboard. If wire is used, give it a final twist with pliers, and when using thread, tie the knot so that there is no slack in the thread.

Illustration No. 31. *Framed roses.*

The roses must fit snugly against the velvet so that they don't wobble. Repeat until all the flowers are in place.

For the buds, cut a groove in the side of each and place a piece of wire in the groove. Brush on hot wax until the hole is filled and the wire is sealed to the bud. Then thread the ends of the wire through the holes in the velvet, just as you did with the roses.

Any lightweight material such as fern, plastic leaves, or even wax leaves can be glued to the velvet as the arrangement is being put in place.

When the arrangement is completed, again brush the velvet to re-

Illustration No. 32. *Madonna wall decoration.*

move any bits of wax. Cut any long ends of wire and fasten the frame over the velvet-covered backing. If a sheet of paper is pasted to the back of the frame, you will not only have a neater piece of work but will also eliminate the possibility of the wire ends scratching the wall.

MADONNA WALL DECORATION

The combination of wax figures and plastic flowers also creates an unusual wall hanging. To fasten wax figures to the backing, cut slashes in their backs, insert wire, and then fill the holes with hot wax. When attaching the flowers, wind the wire around the stems in the most inconspicuous places possible. Any other light decorations such as the sequin stars can be glued on. (Illustration No. 32.)

CARVED CANDLES

Hand carved candles can be as elaborate or as plain as your talent and patience allows. Two of the less involved types of carving are shown in Illustration No. 33. It is also possible to carve a block candle into intricate shapes just as you would carve soap or plaster. Such candles are generally a labor of love since they are so time-consuming. They are not commercially feasible unless a mold is made so that they can be reproduced.

Unless you are exceptionally talented, all carving should begin with a design on paper. Graph paper is of enormous help when repeating patterns or making geometric designs. A completed design can be transferred to the candle by tracing over it with a ball-point pen, pressing hard enough so that indentations are clearly visible in the wax. Following the traced lines, gently dig out the wax with a knife or carving tool.

The technique for the candle with the frog and mushrooms is more a matter of outlining a design than really carving. Using an X-Acto knife, cut narrow grooves along the traced outline. Don't attempt to make straight cuts but, rather, cut toward the center on each side of the line so that the finished groove is V-shaped.

The carved lines were painted to make the carving stand out, but this would not be necessary if the candle were poured in two colors and the cuts were made down to the second color.

There is an inexpensive ceramic tool that is very helpful in making clean carving lines. In fact, it is two tools on one handle because there are different tools at each end. My favorite is the lace tool, which has a needle point on one end and a sort of curved, pointed scoop on

Illustration No. 33. *Carved candles.*

the other. The needle point is good for detail work, and the scoop end cleans and smooths the carved lines.

The raised flowers on the other candle are made by cutting away a portion of the candle so that the design is in relief. Begin by making shallow carvings over all the traced lines to sharply define the design.

Then scrape away the wax outside the design in as high or low relief as wanted. If the raised portion is at least one-fourth of an inch high, it will allow more freedom in carving the flowers and leaves. Variations in height and depth of carving will be more pleasing that a flat, carved surface.

When carving the petals, vary the depth of the carving. Have some of the petals with thin tips and some with raised tips. Cut some with indentations in the middle and some that taper on the sides and are raised in the middle. Cut fairly deep around the centers of the flowers and then round them slightly. There should be no sharp angles in the flowers themselves, only around the edges of the petals and leaves.

Treat the leaves in the same manner. Carve some so that they overlap other leaves and undercut portions of the leaf edges so that they appear quite thin. After all the relief carving has been completed, cut veins in the petals and leaves.

After the design is finished, the next thing that needs attention is the candle. Scrape away the wax from around the design. The area adjacent to the design should be flat and smooth with no evidence of the carving being visible on the candle itself. In order to achieve such a surface, it will be necessary to remove some wax all the way to the top, bottom, and sides of the candle, thus reducing the diameter of the candle slightly.

When the candle is as smooth as it is possible to make it with knives and other tools, scrub it briskly with a piece of nylon net to remove as many marks and nicks as possible. Brush off any loose wax and polish with a soft cloth or nylon hose.

A small, stiff-bristled brush is almost a necessity when carving in wax. It will get down into the crevices and remove loose wax particles, keeping the carved area and the surrounding surface clean.

CLAY MOLDS

The use of a clay mold won't even come close to releasing a candle with a surface as perfect as one poured in a metal or glass mold. However, when it comes to unusual shapes and patterns, the clay mold is in a class by itself. The sand-cast candles started the trend toward the more earthy, primitive type of candles, and the clay molds are a further step in this direction.

A clay mold is a one-time mold because the candle is not taken out of the mold. Instead, the mold is removed from the candle by merely pulling it away from the surface. If a ceramic-type clay is used for the mold-making, it can be reused indefinitely. When the clay becomes hard, put it in a rust-proof container and cover it with water. The clay will absorb the water and become soft and pliable again. I usually have three or four pans of clay around in various stages of regeneration.

The clay should be rolled to a uniform thickness of at least one-half inch and preferably an inch. The easiest way to get this uniform thickness is to either glue or nail two wood strips to a flat surface. The thickness of the wood strips will determine the thickness of the rolled clay. The strips should parallel each other, and the distance between them will govern the height or circumference of the finished candle.

When the wood strips are firmly in place, put waxed paper between them and put the clay on top of the paper. With your hands wedge the clay between the pieces of wood as compactly as possible. Next you will need a round, smooth object that is long enough to reach across the two wood strips. I find a tall candle makes an excellent clay rolling pin. Roll this back and forth along the wood strips until the clay is smooth and well packed.

The clay is now ready for decorating. Designs can either be cut in the clay or clay appliqués applied to the surface. If a design is cut into the clay, it will protrude on the finished candle, while a raised design will have the reverse effect.

There is almost no limit to the things that can be partially embedded in the clay. The only thing to remember is that the wax must have something to stick to if the decoration is to become part of the finished candle. Therefore, don't push the decoration all the way into the clay.

A bottom will have to be made for the mold, and this will require rolling another piece of clay. Remove the clay from between the wood strips and peal off the waxed paper. The purpose of the waxed paper was to keep the clay from sticking to the wood. Trim the top and bottom of the clay and bring the two sides together to form a circle. Press the edges together and smooth the joining line with your finger. If the mold is large enough to slip your hand inside, do the same thing to the inside line. If not, use a stick or a spoon to smooth this line.

Roll some strips of clay in your hand and cover the outside of the mold where the two sides joined. This will reinforce the mold and keep it from popping open or leaking when wax is poured into it.

Next, place this clay cylinder on top of the other piece of clay. Roll more strips and place them around the bottom edge of the mold, smoothing the clay so that there are no holes for the wax to leak out. The wick can be inserted in the center of the bottom of the mold before the sides are attached.

If the clay is very wet, it may not be able to support is own weight and will sag out of shape. Clay air dries fairly rapidly, so wait until the clay is dry enough to hold its own shape but still pliable enough to be formed into a circle without breaking.

It is also possible to put a sheet of thin, flexible plastic between the wood strips before rolling the clay and then removing the plastic along with the clay. The clay will stick to the plastic and the clay, and plastic can be rolled together and taped with Scotch or masking tape.

If you want something other than a straight, round candle, the clay mold can be punched, poked, pulled, and twisted into any shape you might wish.

Pour the wax into the mold and refill as for any other candle. When the candle is hard, pull the clay away from it. If there are pieces of clay stuck to the candle, they can be removed under running water with a brush.

Throw the clay into some water, and in several days it will be ready for more mold-making.

6
Weddings and Anniversaries

Holiday candles are seasonal and enjoy only a short life-span each year, but wedding candles are in demand 365 days a year. There always seems to be a scarcity of attractive wedding and anniversary candles, and this is a void waiting to be filled by the skilled candlemaker.

WEDDING PAIR

If there is to be a centerpiece of flowers on the table, as well as candles, it is necessary to balance the arrangement with two candles rather than having only one. The matched pair in Illustration No. 34 can be put together in a very short time.

Cover the candles and bases with whipped wax and add sprays of lily of the valley toward the top and bottom of the candles. Arrange four plastic bells between the lilies of the valley and scatter small flowers over the base. The bride and groom can be poured in wax and painted, or for even more ease in decorating, the wedding couple can come from the large stock of a cake-decorating supply house.

The frosted effect on the candles is obtained by dipping them after the wax is applied. If the candles are to be dipped, this should be done before they are attached to the bases. The bases can be fastened to the candle, covered with whipped wax, and then dipped.

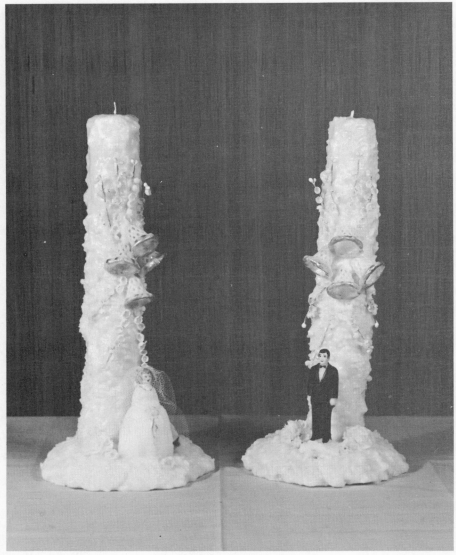

Illustration No. 34. *Wedding pair.*

WEDDING TAPERS

If you have plenty of time and patience, you can dip your own tapers, but since both of those virtues are in short supply as far as I'm concerned, the tapers in Illustration No. 35 were supplied by a store.

The tapers were decorated with Whip Wax and a cake-decorating tool. The bells and lily of the valley were inserted in the wax, and the wax was sprinkled with gold glitter to match the gold holder. The bottom portion of the tapers should be covered thickly with wax about halfway up the candle, but there should be no wax on the portion of the taper which fits into the holder. Starting from the middle of the candle, make swirls up the sides with the cake tool.

Illustration No. 35. *Wedding tapers.*

Illustration No. 36. *Bible and rings.*

Pour a round slab of wax about one-fourth of an inch thick and cover it with Whip Wax. Press a bride and groom into the wax and place the wax circle in the center of the candleholder.

A low bowl filled with fresh flowers could be substituted for the bride and groom. If desired, the outside of the bowl could be covered with Whip Wax to match the tapers.

BIBLE AND RINGS

A wedding and engagement ring from the dime store sets the theme for the candle in Illustration No. 36. The rings were tied with thin white satin ribbon, and the stem of an orange blossom was stuck in each knot to cover it. The other ends of the ribbon were pinned to the front of the candle. A wax bible was placed over the pins and fastened to the candle with hot wax. The ribbon was then brought over the top and down the front of the bible. Three orange blossoms were placed at the top of the bible.

A ruffle was made of white net and pinned in a circle on the bottom portion of the candle. When fastening the net circle to the candle, leave a hole in the center. In other words, don't cover the candle completely with the net. Lily of the valley and small roses were pinned so that they formed a spray in front of the net. The bare spot in the center of the net circle was filled with whipped wax, which covered the stems of the roses and lily of the valley, and a white wax orchid was pushed into the whipped wax.

The center of the orchid and the binding on the bible can be painted either gold or silver to match the rings.

WEDDING COUPLE

The base for this candle requires two sizes of cake pans. If all your cake pans are the same size, pour and remove one base and then pour the other. When the wax from the last pouring is firm, cut a circle in the wax, using a paper pattern which is approximately one inch smaller than the pan. When wax is hard, it will be easy to remove the cut circle. Attatch the two circles of wax with the smaller circle on top and then fasten to the candle.

Cover a plastic lattice heart frame with small flowers and leaves. Stems can be threaded through the latticework to hold flowers in place, and the flowers positioned so that all the stems are concealed. At the bottom front of the candle fasten a runner of white velvet or satin ribbon and bring it down to the bottom of the base. The ribbon can be secured to the base at various points with minute pieces of adhesive. Cover the top circle of the base, except for the ribbon, with Whip Wax. An edging of Whip Wax may be placed along the sides of the ribbon to hold it in place if necessary.

Put the flower-covered heart against the front of the candle and add more wax to hold it in place. Adhesive, hot wax, pins, or an electric

Illustration No. 37. *Wedding couple.*

needle can be used at the top of the heart to fasten it securely to the candle. Using a small amount of Whip Wax, attach two small bells directly beneath the top of the heart. Press the bride and groom into Whip Wax in front of the heart and scatter flowers in a semi-circle around the top portion of the base. With a cake-decorating tool make scallops around the outside edges of the base with Whip Wax. (Illustration No. 37.)

CLASPED HANDS

The white seaweed which is used as a background for the bells is available at cake-decorating supply houses. It comes in various widths like ribbon and is perfect for a light, frothy decoration on wedding candles.

The clasped hands are from a plastic mold and were poured in the

Illustration No. 38. *Clasped hands.*

palest of pink waxes. The tips of the bride's sleeve, the groom's coat and shirt cuff, and the ring were painted. If desired, small rhinestones can be set in the ring with adhesive.

A spray of white fern and lily of the valley was pinned to the candle, and a seaweed bow was placed over the fern. The plastic bells were placed on the candle so that they seem to hang from the bow, and a plastic dove was glued to the top of the bells. Another dove was fastened to the side of the candle, and the clasped hands were fastened near the bottom. The hands should be warmed before being attached so that they can be shaped to the contour of the candle. A final touch of white carnations and fern circled the bottom of the candle. (Illustration No. 38.)

WEDDING INVITATION

The first question people ask when seeing one of these candles is "How did you transfer the printing to the candle?" It is a logical question because that's what seems to have happened. As with many things in candlemaking, however, it's not nearly so complicated.

The wedding invitation is cut, leaving a half-inch border around the printing. It is then dipped in hot wax and pinned to the candle. Presto! The printing is transferred to the candle. If very hot wax is used for the dip, it soaks through the paper and also coats the outside, making it appear as though only the printing is on the candle and not on a piece of paper.

Wedding invitations seem to come in all shapes and sizes these days, and you have to adjust the decorating to fit the invitation. In Illustration No. 39, one of the invitations was almost as tall as the candle, and so the decorations were arranged accordingly. There wasn't enough room to cluster bells at the top of the invitation, so they were placed along the side. I have had invitations so wide that they wrapped completely around the candle; those kind present decorating problems.

After the paper has been pinned to the candle, cover all the edges with whipped wax and stick in the wax flowers, bells, and leaves. The roses will fit closer to the candle and look better if the bottom of the flower is flattened by cutting off some of the wax.

Possibly because they are personalized, these candles keep selling and selling. In fact, they are the most popular wedding candles I have ever made. Brides ask to have them made and then use them for the announcement party and on through to the reception. After being packed away most of the year, they are brought out again when the anniversary date comes around. They also make very popular gifts, and all brides seem delighted to receive them.

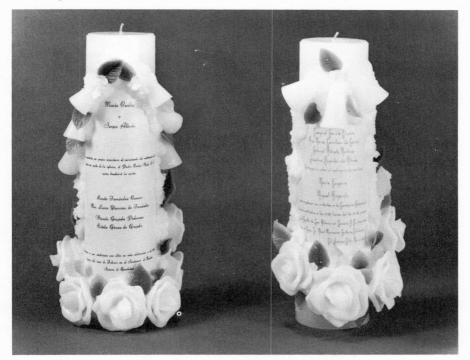

Illustration No. 39. *Wedding invitations.*

If a supply of leaves, bells, and roses is poured up during a slack period, one of these candles can be assembled in about ten minutes. If you are curious about what to charge, they retail here for $10.00.

There is another way to make these candles, which is more time consuming, but for somebody special you might like to try it. Most craft shops have an acrylic transfer medium that will enable you to use only the printing on the candle without using the paper. This material produces a transparent decal and will absorb the ink from a picture in a magazine or from printed matter. Only the colors are visible, and the surrounding areas are transparent.

WEDDING BELLS

The detail on the wedding candle in Illustration No. 40 is not too clear because of the difficulty in photographing an all-white candle. Everything has a tendency to sort of blur together.

This candle was to be used as part of a flower arrangement, so the bottom portion was left undecorated. If it is to stand alone, the decorations can extend the full length of the candle.

The bells were placed in a bed of whipped wax, and then the white roses were fitted around the bells. A thin layer of soft wax was poured on a piece of waxed paper, and the ribbons cut from the wax. Place the ribbons on a heating pad while working with them so that they will stay warm and be pliable enough to bend and twist without breaking. Cut some short lengths of ribbon and bend the ends together to make bows. Place the bows at the top of the candle above the bells. Then add the ribbons, twisting then and fastening to the bells where they touch to lessen the possibility of breakage.

Illustration No. 40. *Wedding and anniversary candles.*

There are none on this candle, but I often pour small birds in pale blue wax to represent the bluebird of happiness.

The candle can be made more personal by using something that will be part of the wedding. In this case, the bride had her dress made, and pieces of lace were cut from the dress material, dipped in wax, and applied to the bells. The lace was then highlighted in gold. Occasionally, another thing I do with these candles is to work in the colors of the bridesmaids' dresses.

ANNIVERSARY BELLS

The anniversary candle in Illustration No. 40 was made in much the same manner as the wedding candle. The "50" was cut from a wax sheet and fastened to the candle while it was still warm. All the decorations were held in place with whipped wax, and whipped wax was placed on the candle so that it formed a circular frame around the numerals. The numerals were painted gold, and then gold glitter was sprinkled on while the paint was wet. After the paint had dried, a circle of paper was cut to fit around the numbers and pinned in place. The entire candle was then sprayed with gold paint and the paper removed. The unsprayed area around the numerals provides a light background for the golden "50" so that the numerals are the most prominent piece of decoration on the entire candle.

The bells may be left smooth as they come from the mold or may be embellished by the addition of whipped wax. This is done by putting whipped wax around the bottom portion of the bells only. There should not be a heavy application of wax; it should be put on sparingly.

Whether the bells are used with the whipped wax or left plain, they should always be dipped before being put on a candle. To make the bells hollow, it is necessary to pour out the excess wax after a shell has formed. This often leaves the insides rough and in need of some smoothing. Holding the bell by the bottom edge, dip half the bell in hot wax. After the wax has cooled, repeat the dipping on the other side. This will not only coat the outside of the bell but will coat and smooth the inside also.

ANNIVERSARY CANDLE

For a less elaborate anniversary candle and one that can be put together in a very short time, try the one in Illustration No. 41. The anniversary shield can be bought at most hobby shops that stock candle supplies or at any mail-order candle supplier. Almost any plastic flowers would be appropriate, although white or pastels are better if the flowers are not to be solidly covered with gold. Pin the flowers in place and spray

Illustration No. 41. *Anniversary candle.*

A cone candle decorated with roses and grapes.

All-wax decorations of roses, leaves and grapes.

the candle and decorations with gold paint. To get a misty gold effect, hold the spray can at least two or three feet from the candle.

When the gold has dried, pin the shield in place and cover the stems of the flowers with a gold foil border. Two small love birds beneath the shield will complete the arrangement.

The most complete assortment of items for decorating wedding and anniversary candles can be found at cake decorating supply houses. They have all kinds of bells, wedding couples, flowers, and plastic frames that can make short work of decorating candles for these two special occasions. However, their decorating items are not limited to weddings and anniversaries, and after spending an evening with one of their catalogs, you will probably begin the next day with dozens of new candle ideas spinning around in your head.

7
Valentine, Easter, and Christmas

The arrival of any holiday seems to be a signal to open the pocketbook. People who wouldn't think of spending the money to buy a candle for themselves, willingly buy one for a gift. Just take a stroll through a candle shop a few weeks before a holiday and see how firmly the owners believe in this. Although the bread-and-butter line is still there, the holiday candles occupy the most prominent and conspicuous spots in the shop.

VALENTINE

Only the better candle holidays will be covered here, and we'll start with Valentine's Day. Even a plain red candle is suitable for this occasion, but a little time spent decorating will show that it couldn't be anything but somebody's valentine.

NET HEART

The frame for the net heart is ordinary household wire that is heavy enough to hold its shape but still flexible enough to bend with ease. Bend the wire into an approximate heart shape to determine the correct size and then cut. Straighten the wire and cut four or five strips of net in varying widths about three times the length of the wire. Stack all the strips so that the widest strip is on the bottom and graduate the sizes so that the

Illustration No. 42. *Net heart.*

narrowest piece is on top. Hold the net together and weave the wire through the net. When all the net is on the wire, adjust the ruffle so that it is even and twist the edges of the wire together. Arrange the ruffle so it covers the twisted wire.

Bend the wire into a heart shape again. Pin the heart to the candle and pile whipped wax in the center. Cover the whipped wax center thickly with small flowers, and glue or pin gold foil cherubs and hearts to the top of the candle. The cut edges of the net can be painted with gold, or the entire heart can be gold sprayed lightly before it is fastened to the candle. (Illustration No. 42.)

CHERUBS AND HEARTS

Only a big, fat red candle will do for this one. Pour wax into a pan to a depth of about one half inch and using a paper pattern, cut a heart that is open in the center. Cover the heart with whipped wax and fill in with flowers, leaves, and glitter.

Pour in a plastic mold or cut from a sheet of wax two small hearts and attach them to candle. Outline the hearts by pinning small beads to the candle. Attach the wax cherubs to the sides of the candle, and you have a Valentine candle to perk up any table.

The wax heart may be made without a hole in the center and completely covered with flowers. (Illustration No. 43.)

EASTER

The next important holiday for candlemakers is Easter. The variety of Easter candles is almost as unlimited as the ones for Christmas. When you think of all the Easter symbols you can incorporate into your candlemaking, it's not hard to understand why this is a favorite season for candles. A few of the motifs for decorating are: calla and Easter lilies, Madonnas, lambs, chicks, ducks, rabbits, the cross, and eggs.

Since Easter is a religious holiday, let's do that type of candle first and then go on to egg and rabbit decorations.

BIBLE AND CROSS

When making the candle in Illustration No. 44, a poured base and also a small rectangle of wax for a stand will be needed. A small cardboard box lined with aluminum foil will make an adequate mold for the stand. It isn't necessary that the stand have a perfect finish because it will be covered by the velvet. Cut the rectangle to the desired height if the mold is not the correct size, and then cut or melt one of the ends at an angle so that the top of the stand slants downward.

After attaching the base, place the stand on the base against the front of the candle and make a small mark on the candle at the top of the stand. Lay the velvet on the candle with the pile side against the wax and

Illustration No. 43. *Cherubs and hearts.*

pin or glue the bottom end of the velvet to the candle at the marked spot. Attach stand to candle and bring velvet over the stand, arranging in soft folds.

Paint the cover and bookmark of the bible, and when the paint is dry, place the bible on top of the stand. Pin through the binding of the

Illustration No. 44. *Bible and cross.*

book to the wax stand to hold the book in place. Be sure to cover the pinheads with a dot of wax and paint. Glue can also be used for fastening the bible, but don't even consider using wax. One drop of spilled wax on the velvet and you have to start all over again since it is impossible to remove the wax from the velvet pile.

Starting in the center back of the candle about halfway between the top and bottom, pin lilies down the side of the candle, across the base, and up the other side of the candle. Cover the stems of flowers and the base with whipped wax, being very careful not to splatter any on the velvet. Where the velvet touches the base, cover with whipped wax to hide the raw edges. Paint and glitter the cross and attach it to the candle. (Illustration No. 45.)

Illustration No. 45. *Praying hands.*

The bible is from a plastic mold and the cross can either be poured in a mold or cut from a sheet of wax.

PRAYING HANDS AND CROSS

If the praying hands are substituted for the stand and bible, you have a candle that looks totally different from the previous one but is actually quite similar as far as decorating techniques are concerned.

When the hands are removed from the mold, there will be excess wax on the cuffs from the pouring hole. Utilize this wax as the base or anchor to hold the hands in place in the whipped wax. If it is trimmed off, it will be necessary to cover the cuffs with wax to attach them.

Cover the base with whipped wax and bring the wax up the front of the candle. Insert the praying hands in the whipped wax. Mass the lilies around the sides and front of the candle so that the hands appear to be rising from the lilies.

The large plastic lilies are fairly heavy, and their weight causes them to slide out of the whipped wax. When a number of them are used, as in this candle, it is better to pin them securely to the candle and base. Then gently move the petals and drop whipped wax around the stems to cover. (Illustration No. 45.)

LARGE CROSS

For a large, impressive Easter candle, make the candle in a cross cake pan. (Illustration No. 46.) Check the pan carefully before pouring to be certain there are no dents or undercuts which would prevent removal of the candle.

Pour the cake pan half-full of wax and let it harden. Center a wick on the top of the wax and brush with hot wax to hold in place. If the pan will never be used for anything but making candles, a small hole can be punched in the center of the top of the pan and a wick threaded through the hole. If the pan is to serve double-duty, I am sure you would prefer not to have cake mix leaking out of the hole. In this case, run the wick at the top of the candle up the side of the mold and over the top, and hold in place on the outside of mold with a bit of clay or adhesive. Pour the other half of the mold. When the wick is pulled away from the wax on the completed candle, there will be a small groove across half of the top, but this can be filled in by brushing on hot wax.

The candle can be textured with a comb after it is removed from the mold to give it a weathered appearance. Painting with dark brown antiquing paint (available at hobby and ceramic shops) and wiping

Illustration No. 46. *Large cross.*

down with a soft, clean cloth will leave a darker color in the indentations, giving the candle a wood tone.

Place the candle on its back on a piece of waxed paper and fill in the area between the bottom of the cross and the arm of the cross with whipped wax. Also put whipped wax on the bottom front of the candle and on the front of the arm. Insert lilies in the whipped wax and allow the wax to harden. When putting the flowers near the bottom of the cross, be sure they do not extend below the candle. If they do, the candle will not stand straight.

When all the wax has hardened, remove the waxed paper from the back of the candle. The wax at the back that was against the paper will be mashed flat, and a coating of whipped wax should be placed over it to give it the same fluffy appearance as the front.

STAINED GLASS WINDOW

The simulated leading in the stained glass window was made from flexible lead strips available at most hobby shops. These strips can be cut with scissors and bend easily into almost any shape.

Bend two long strips to form an arch and glue to candle. Next, cut strips from the cross and join them together. The strips will fit together more smoothly if the corners and other places of joining are mitered (cut on an angle). Fill in the rest of the window with strips cut in any pattern desired.

When all the lead strips have been glued in place, paint each section to represent stained glass. Glass paints are particularly good for this, but oils or other paints may be used.

Outline the robe of the Madonna in gold and place her in front of the window. Put lilies beside and behind her and then dip base in hot wax until the hot wax barely covers the top of base. This will fasten the Madonna and flowers to the base very securely. (Illustration No. 47.)

There are other ways to get stained glass effects on candles. One is to cut pieces of colored cellophane to represent the glass panes. Another is to combine wax and waxed paper. Brush a coat of wax on a piece of waxed paper, put another piece of waxed paper over this, and press with a warm iron. The heat will fuse the paper to the wax, and the panes can then be cut to any size needed. Thin pieces of plastic can also be painted on one side and then glued to the candle.

Hurricane candles are particularly well suited to this type of decoration because of the effect of the light shining through the stained glass panels.

MADONNA AND LEAVES

An arrangement of plastic leaves, calla lilies, and a Madonna in Illustration No. 47 adds the Easter touch to this simple but pleasing candle.

Attach leaves to the candle so they form a half circle and then fasten lilies to the leaves and base with hot wax. Place the Madonna in the center of the candle, so that the leaves and lilies form a frame behind her.

EASTER EGGS

There are available regular plaster and plastic molds of eggs that

Illustration No. 47. *Madonna arrangements.*

can be used for Easter, but if you want a number of molds for a small price go to the local dime store. The hollow plastic eggs made to hold candy and other goodies for children are usually in sets of three or four sizes. This plastic is hard enough to take fairly hot wax, and the hard surface results in a smooth candle.

It will be necessary to cut or drill a hole in the small end of the mold

Illustration No. 48. *Egg candles.*

for the wick and another larger hole in the bottom for pouring. It will also be necessary to build a small wall of clay around the bottom of the mold, so when it is poured, it will stand upright. The clay wall can be eliminated if the mold is placed in a wide-mouthed glass jar or glass. The two mold pieces fit together like a box, and the sides must be sealed so the wax won't leak out. Another way to use these molds is to pour them in two sections and join the two parts of the candle together with either whipped wax or hot wax.

Regardless of which method is used, there will be a seam line on the

Illustration No. 49. *Window candle.*

candle that must be covered. Whipped wax studded with sequins, glitter, or small flowers provides an effective camouflage.

In Illustration No. 48, the seam line was concealed with a row of sequins. A spray of pansies was curved from the bottom of the candle up along the side. Two wax butterflies and a cluster of flowers on the opposite side complete this easy-to-decorate candle.

On the other candle in Illustration No. 48, a strip of pearls was placed over the seam. A portion of the back of the wax rabbit was melted off so that it would fit flush against the candle. A circle of gold foil became a frame around the bunny, and gold foil sprays were glued on each side of the frame. The final touch was the addition of small roses and sequined birds.

In Illustration No. 49, a window candle is made from the egg mold. Separate the mold and pour wax in each half. If there are holes in the mold for wick and pouring, cover these holes with electricians' tape, adhesive, or modeling clay before pouring. One of the half-molds should be filled with wax but pour out the center wax in the other half after the thickness of the wall has reached approximately one-fourth of an inch. Cut a hole in this shell large enough to insert the decoration.

When candle halves have been removed from the molds, lay a wick lengthwise in the center of the solid half and seal in place by brushing with hot wax. Place the two sides of the egg together and attach by brushing hot wax around the seam line several times or by running a soldering gun or electric needle along the seam line.

Lay the egg on its back and pour hot wax through the hole until the shell is about half-full. This seals the two sides completely and furnishes a better background for decorating. Contrast is provided if this pouring is made in a color different from the candle.

After the wax has hardened, glue a row of sequins along the side of candle to cover the seam line. Scatter other sequins over the candle and fasten with glue. A portion of a gold foil medallion was glued to the inside of the candle. A full length wax Madonna was cut in half and placed inside the candle on a bed of whipped wax. A spray of gold foil leaves was glued around the opening and two wax calla lilies attached to the bottom of the candle with whipped wax.

The decorating possibilities of this candle are endless. The decorations inside the window can be anything that strikes your fancy. Small figures, a bouquet of small flowers, or even a tiny crèche for Christmas are all possibilities. The window can become the frame for a favorite snapshot or photograph, or a picture cut from a magazine could form the background for unusual decorating.

The egg candles are as attractive resting on their sides as they are standing upright. On the horizontal egg in Illustration No. 50, pearl strips were used to cover the seam line, and four short strips were brought up from the seam to within about one inch of the wick. The wick was inserted after the candle was poured, and a long wick left at the top.

The bottom of the rose must be flattened either by melting or cutting. Then put it on the top of the candle to determine where the leaves

Illustration No. 50. *Egg and rose candle.*

and buds should be placed but don't attach permanently. Fasten the leaves and buds to the top and sides of the candle, being careful to cover the ends of the pearl strips and to leave a blank area around the wick. Poke a hole through the rose, thread the wick through the hole, and fasten the rose to the candle.

A word of caution—only wax flowers and leaves should be used on this candle because the decorations come in direct contact with the flame.

Illustration No. 51. *Egg tree.*

EGG TREE

The egg tree has been written up before, but because of inquiries about it, a picture is being included this time. A cone mold, egg shells, and artificial flowers are all that are needed for an egg tree.

Crack the egg shells gently on one side and carefully peel away the

Illustration No. 52. *Bunny family.*

shell until there is a hole large enough for removing the egg. Rinse the inside of the shell with a mixture of vinegar and water. This candle requires thirty or forty eggs; so it may take some time to save the necessary eggshells.

When enough shells have been collected to make pouring worthwhile, line them up with the hole side up and stick each one in a small piece

113

of clay or adhesive so that they won't tip over. Pour hot wax in different colors and when the wax has hardened, peel the shells away from the wax.

The eggs do not have to be perfectly round; so it isn't necessary to pour the wax all the way to the hole. However, try to pour about the same amount of wax in each shell so that the eggs will be of a uniform thickness. The eggs can be all the same size or various sizes. If they are different sizes, use the largest at the bottom and graduate to the smallest at the top. The eggs will probably need a hot wax dip before they are put on the candle.

When the candle is poured, leave a long wick at the top. Begin at the bottom of the candle and cover a portion with whipped wax. The candle will be more more symmetrical if the eggs are placed around the candle rather than up and down the sides. There will be spaces between the eggs no matter how carefully they are aligned, and these spaces can be filled with flowers or tiny wax-coated candy eggs.

The eggs can be decorated with glitter, paint, or decals, but the eggs and flowers are really all the decoration needed for this candle. (Illustration No. 51.)

BUNNY FAMILY

Pour the bunny family and birds in pastel colors and paint in the features. Mama rabbit has a flower hat on top of her head, and a tiny pearl choker was attached with rubber cement. Papa rabbit is holding an egg that is stuck in his arms with adhesive. The small eggs are candy eggs from the dime store that have been stuck on toothpicks and dipped in hot wax.

Cover the base with whipped wax and place the rabbits in the wax along with the flower sprays behind them. Build a nest of whipped wax and fill it with little candy eggs. The eggs can be held together with adhesive. Cover the base with flowers and attach the birds to the side of the candle. (Illustration No. 52.)

CHRISTMAS CANDLES

Christmas is *the* season for all candlemakers and for some the only season. There are candlecrafters who work on Christmas candles all year so they will have a tremendous stock for the holiday buyers. Whether the candles are made year-round or just before Thanksgiving, there is always a market for the Christmas candle.

There are so many things that can be used to decorate Christmas

Illustration No. 53. *Bells and poinsettias.*

candles that it's sometimes hard to decide between all the available orna-
ments. Decorations are more restrained for candles to be displayed during the year, but on Christmas candles almost anything goes. Large
amounts of gold, glitter, and tinsel on any other candles would be in
poor taste, but for Christmas it seems to be the more the better.

BELLS AND POINSETTIAS

Where would the candlemaker be without plastic? Not only are some of our molds made of plastic, but the plastic decorations seem to multiply each year. Besides doing much to enhance a plain candle, plastic decorations have the added attraction of speeding up decorating time. I know of one shop that specializes in plastic flower-decorated candles. Although they stock a few other kinds of candles from commercial candle companies, the ones made in the shop are all decorated with plastic flowers, and they sell almost as fast as they are finished.

In Illustration No. 53, the candle is decorated entirely with plastic items. A strip of the versatile seaweed was sprayed gold and pinned to the front of the candle, so that it formed a large circle. Plastic holly leaves were pinned behind and in front of the seaweed. Plastic bells were sprayed lightly with gold and then with gold glitter and fastened on top of the seaweed. Next, the plastic poinsettias were sprayed with glitter glue, sprinkled with red glitter, and attached to the candle by making a hole in the wax with a hot ice pick. Not counting the drying time for the gold paint, this candle can be decorated in about ten minutes.

BRANDY SNIFTER ARRANGEMENTS

These come under the heading of wax Christmas decorations rather than candles, but they do have a place on the candlemaker's shelf. If a $2.00 or $3.00 item is needed to offset some of the more expensive candles, these container arrangements can fill that need.

A dull glass container detracts a great deal from these arrangements; so the first step should be to polish the glass until it sparkles. After the arrangement is completed, polish the glass again to remove any stray bits of wax or any fingerprints.

The waving Santa in Illustration No. 54 is in a very small snifter, and the decorations are scaled accordingly. Cover the bottom of the glass with whipped wax and then build up a small mound of wax for Santa to sit on. Place Santa on top of the wax mound. Put tiny pine burs in the wax on one side of him and pine needle clusters on the other. Cover the stem and foot of the glass with whipped wax and insert holly leaves, berries, and pine needle clusters. Sprinkle glitter over the wax in the snifter and also over the whipped wax around the bottom of the glass.

For a larger arrangement, such as the Madonna in Illustration No. 55, pliers, tweezers, or kitchen tongs are helpful in putting the decorations in place. Trying to do this with your fingers sometimes results in more decorations being knocked out of place than being set in place.

Illustration No. 54. *Waving Santa.*

Cover the bottom of the glass with whipped wax and put small roses in the wax at the front. Stick foil leaves in the wax on each side of the container and some fern sprays in the back. Lower the Madonna into the center of the glass, pressing it down firmly to be certain it is securely fastened. Cover the rim with a gold foil border and the foot of the glass with pieces of a foil medallion.

117

Illustration No. 55. *Madonna in glass.*

In Illustration No. 56, the praying hands have been made the center of interest. Cover the bottom of the glass with whipped wax and bend two pine branches to follow the contour of the container. Twine Christmas beads through the branches and place them in the wax against the sides of the glass. If there is a problem with the branches staying where they are put, clip them to the sides of the glass with clothespins until the wax has hardened enough to hold them. Using kitchen tongs or pliers, place the flowers in the wax at the front and back of the glass. Add more whipped wax so that all the stems of the flowers are covered and press the hands in the center of the flowers.

Illustration No. 56. *Praying hands.*

Illustration No. 57. *Santa Claus head.*

CONE SANTA

It's impossible to verify, but there is a strong suspicion that the first candlecrafter to get hold of a cone mold immediately made a Santa Claus. Every candlemaker since then has had the same urge when pouring a cone candle. The different ways to make a Santa candle with this mold seem to be endless, and Illustration No. 57 shows yet another variation.

Pour the candle in white or very pale pink. Paint the portion for the hat a bright red and top with a whipped wax ball. Possibly a string of discarded beads might be used for the beard, but they are seldom long enough. Christmas beads are a good size, and there are usually enough beads in one length to make several beards. To obtain the correct length, it is generally necessary to cut the beads, and that presents the problem of how to keep the beads from slipping off the string. One easy solution is to take the cut end of the string, bring it down under the first bead, and tie the end of the string and the body of the string together under the bead.

Begin on the side of the candle at the bottom of the hat and loop the beads up and down around the face to form a beard. Put a pin through the string at the top of each loop to hold in place. To hold the first and last bead of the beard in place, you can fasten with hot wax or whipped wax or dig a small hole, heat the wax with a hot ice pick or electric needle, and insert the beads in the holes. Whatever method is used, arrange the holly leaves so that these beads are covered. Place a single string of beads along the top of the beard for a mustache.

Dig out holes in the wax for the eyes and nose. Either heat the wax in these holes or drop in hot wax and immediately insert two small blue balls for the eyes and a large red ball for the nose. Substitute holly leaves for fur on the hat by pinning a row of leaves all around the candle.

An alternative to the bead beard is a holly beard. Pin holly leaves vertically on the lower portion of the face, and when the beard is full and bushy, add some horizontally positioned leaves for a mustache.

SANTA AND REINDEER

The candle in Illustration No. 58 was the answer to a request for a pair of candles to put on either side of a fireplace. They are large, about three feet tall, and the floor is about the only place where they don't look ridiculous. However, the candle can be scaled down to table size by putting the sled closer to the bottom and having fewer reindeer.

The Santa, sled, and reindeer are all made of wax, but appropriate ones can also be obtained in plastic. The candle was textured by dipping crumpled paper toweling into partially cooled wax and pressing the paper lightly against the candle. The flame from a propane torch was then passed lightly over the surface of the candle. This makes the texturing adhere better to the candle and also blends the colors when more than one is used. If desired, bronzing powder may be brushed on the raised portions of the texturing before the torch is used.

To make the snow trail, place small U-shaped pieces of wire in a spiral around the candle. This gives the whipped wax a base to hang onto and holds it in place so that it can be made wide enough to accommodate the reindeer. Put the whipped wax on in sections, holding the candle in a horizontal position. When one section has hardened, go on to another.

Illustration No. 58. *Santa and reindeer.*

Illustration No. 59. *Santa in swing.*

It is practically impossible to complete the spiral around the candle at one time because the whipped wax keeps dropping off as the candle is turned.

When the snow trail is completed and the wax has hardened, add more whipped wax and place the reindeer in the wax. Press the sides of the reindeer against the candle and fasten with whipped wax as added insurance against breakage of the reindeer's fragile legs. Attach Santa to the sled and put the sled at the bottom of the whipped wax spiral. Loop small gold cord around the necks of the reindeer to represent the reins and fasten the end of the cord to the sled with a pin.

SANTA IN A SWING

Pour a tree stump mold in a wood tone and stick several pieces of wire in the side of the candle. Cover the wire with whipped wax the same color as the candle to form a branch. If you don't have a stump mold, a fairly realistic tree stump can be made by pouring a round candle and covering it with whipped wax. Press the whipped wax against the candle until it loses its roughness and becomes fairly smooth, and make indentations in the wax with your fingers so the candle won't be perfectly round. Dig grooves and lines in the wax with the end of a brush handle, piece of wire, or any other object that will give you the effect you want. Since it's impossible to predict just what the end result of all this pressing and grooving will be, it's hard to say whether the candle would be improved by dipping. If you would like a smoother candle, by all means dip, but if you want it rough, leave it alone.

Holes were punched in the swing seat and in Santa's hands. Small gold cord was threaded through the holes, and the two ends of the cord were pinned to the top of the tree branch. The top of the stump, the base, and also the tree branch were covered with white whipped wax. The whipped wax should cover the ends of the cord and the pins. A spray of pine branches and holly were placed by the side of the candle, and pine burr clusters were scattered over the snow on the base.

Most candles just sit, but this one suggests movement, and most people can't resist giving Santa a slight push to see if he will really swing. He will. (Illustration No. 59.)

MADONNA ARRANGEMENT

Bubble branches can be bought at a wholesale florist, or you can make them yourself. The ones in Illustration No. 60 were made by cutting ten pieces of wire of various lengths and bending them into the desired shapes. The wire was then coated with glue and dipped into a container of plastic bubbles. It may be necessary to use two or more coatings of the glue and bubbles to get the thickness needed.

Cover the back of the base with whipped wax and stick in three plastic feathers cut in different lengths. When using plastic flowers or foliage with a wire stem, it is easy to make them stand upright if the wire is bent

Illustration No. 60. *Madonna arrangement.*

at a ninety-degree angle about one inch from the bottom and formed into a circle. This circle makes a base that the wax can stick to, and even fairly heavy decorations can be handled successfully in this manner. Arrange the feathers so that they branch out from the candle.

Put some of the longer lengths of bubble-covered wire and also some

125

tall leaf sprays at the back of the candle and to the side. Cover one side of base with whipped wax, and using taller pieces toward the back, insert the rest of the bubble branches in the base. Fill in the arrangement with some Christmas beads on wire and small leaf sprays.

Place the Madonna in front of the candle. Build up a mound of whipped wax beside the figure and insert small plastic bells, so that they

Illustration No. 61. *Madonna and sea fan.*

curve slightly toward the front of the base. Cut a piece of plastic feather and insert it horizontally in the whipped wax in front of the Madonna, so that it extends slightly out from the base. Pin large sequin stars on the front of the candle.

MADONNA AND SEA FAN

Illustration No. 61 shows another candle using the same Madonna figure. Sea fan and cattails are not usually thought of as Christmas decorations, but they adapt quite well.

Spray a piece of sea fan with glitter glue and sprinkle heavily with gold glitter. Attach fan to base with whipped wax and put a few small pieces of adhesive on the back of the fan to hold it against the side of the candle until the whipped wax has hardened. Place the Madonna in whipped wax in front of the fan.

Spray small cattails with glue and sprinkle with gold glitter. Place them on each side of the figure and put different-sized Christmas balls around the base of the candle. Place a row of pine needle clusters around the outside edge of the base and a half circle of clusters in front of the Madonna. Scatter tiny Christmas beads over the base and sprinkle the whipped wax thickly with glitter.

CHRISTMAS CAROUSEL

The kids have their merry-go-rounds with prancing ponies, but the older generation can have a Christmas carousel with prancing reindeer.

Leave a long wick when pouring the candle. To make the peaked roof, cut a circle from heavy paper or tagboard. Make a slit in the circle and lap the ends over to make a shallow cone. Staple or tape the cut ends and oil the outside of the cone. Cover the top with a layer of whipped wax and let it harden. Then peel the paper from the wax. Place a peaked mound of whipped wax on top of the candle, cut a small hole in the roof for the wick, and press the roof onto the whipped wax mound. When the wax has hardened, turn the candle upside down and coat the underside of the roof with a layer of whipped wax.

Cover the base with whipped wax and insert Christmas balls and beads. Stick small poinsettias into the wax all around the outside edge of the base. Cut four pieces of coat hanger wire, discarded plastic flower stems, or even pipe cleaners and dip them into hot wax several times. Insert the rods into holes cut in the back of each reindeer. Stick the other end of the rod into the whipped wax roof and fasten reindeer to the side of the candle. If more wax is needed to securely attach the rods to the

Illustration No. 62. *Christmas carousel.*

roof, add it now. Drape a string of Christmas beads around the roof of the carousel and hold in place with pins. Cover the pin heads and a portion of the beads with whipped wax. (Illustration No. 62.)

SNOW FAMILY

This little snow family is easily made by rolling three balls of soft wax for each one. Stack the ball with the largest on the bottom and graduate to the smallest for the head. Roll a long strip of wax for the arms, cut to fit each body, and attach. Make the books by cutting rectangles of wax and bending in the middle.

The scarf for Papa is made by cutting a rectangle of soft wax and winding it around his neck. Mama's bonnet is made from a crescent-

Illustration No. 63. *Snow family.*

shaped piece of wax, and the ribbon can either be made of wax or painted on. Two small flattened balls of wax become the earmuffs for junior. The snowmen should be dipped to cover the minor imperfections and for better adhesion. If the snowmen are painted before being dipped, the paint will have a waxy appearance, and there will be no problem with it chipping off.

If you prefer not to model the snowmen, take different sizes of styrofoam balls and fasten them together with toothpicks. Dip in hot wax until the styrofoam is well coated with wax. Then make the arms, book, scarf, hat, and earmuffs of wax and fasten to the balls.

Cover the base with whipped wax and put a small plastic Christmas tree on one side of the candle and a bubble branch on the other. Place the snow family in front of the candle and put a few holly leaves around the front of the base. Plastic bubbles can be scattered on the candle to represent snowflakes and fastened with glitter cement. Stick a few red holly berries in the base for added color. (Illustration No. 63.)

ANGEL CANDLE

Carve a hole in the candle large enough for the figure to be placed inside. Linoleum carving tools are a help for this, but a sharp knife will do an acceptable job of carving. If whipped wax or texturing is used on the inside of the hole, it is not necessary to worry too much about how smooth the hole is.

In Illustration No. 64, the hole and the surrounding area were textured by dipping paper towels into wax and pressing against the candle. A heavy coating of Treasure Gold was rubbed on all the peaks of the texturing. The bottom of the hole was covered with whipped wax to hold the angel. This was also coated with gold paint. The candle was finished by putting gold foil trim at the top and bottom and gold foil designs on the side and front.

This type of candle can be used for any holiday for just for everyday by putting appropriate decorations on the cut-out.

ANGELS

A base from a star salad mold was covered with whipped wax and two wax angels were placed on either side. A couple of wax birds were perched on the base in front of the candle, and some pine burr clusters were added to the whipped wax.

A bow and ribbon was made from a thin strip of soft wax, and three jeweled wax bells were hung below the bow. Another wax bird was placed in the center of the bow. (Illustration No. 65.)

Illustration No. 64. *Angel candle.*

BELLS AND SINGERS

The candles in Illustration No. 66 were my best sellers last Christmas. The bells are fairly large and are from a plaster mold. Most ceramic shops have a number of bell molds, and it is not hard to find exactly the right size. To make hollow bells, treat them as you would a hur-

Illustration No. 65. *Angels and bells.*

ricane candle and pour out the center wax after a shell has formed around the sides.

Clappers can be made for the bells by putting a large bead on a piece of wire and bending the end of the wire to keep the bead from slipping off. The other end of the wire should be bent, and a circle formed at the end so that it can be anchored in the bell. Dip the bead and wire in hot wax several times and then spray with gold paint. To put the clapper in the bell, turn the bell upside down, pour in a little hot wax or whipped wax and insert the wire in the wax.

The bottom portion of the bells were covered with whipped wax and then dipped and sprayed lightly with gold. To attach decorations this

Illustration No. 66. *Carol singers.*

heavy, place the candle on its back and spoon on just enough low-melting-point whipped wax to hold the bells in place. Leave the candle in this position till the wax has hardened. Fasten the carol singers to the candle in the same manner. When the wax is hard, add more whipped wax around the bells and put the holly leaves and pine cones around the bells and figures. Sprinkle the wax heavily with glitter.

The singers were poured in white and then antiqued. This gives them a mellow appearance and brings out the detail without the bother of painting. The figures were covered with paint, and then the paint was wiped off with a soft cloth. The leaves were outlined in gold and the pine cones brushed with gold.

In Illustration No. 67, all of the candles have bases, and all are composed almost entirely of wax decorations. The angel mold from which the candle with the three angels was made is really a fantastic little mold. Because of the number of parts to the mold, the angels can be short or tall, standing or kneeling. There are a number of hands, and they can

Illustration No. 67. *Christmas candles decorated with wax, beads, jewels, and gold braid.*

be switched around to change the appearance of the angels. Some have books, candles, lanterns, and hands pressed together in prayer.

The pine cones and beads are a variation of the grapes and beads adapted to the Christmas season instead of year-round use.

The trunk of the Christmas tree can be a dowel, juice can, or a short piece of pipe. Whatever it is, when it's covered with whipped wax, only you will know. The decoration on the tree was made by putting on rows of whipped wax and outlining them with gold braid. Large jewels were placed at the points and smaller beads and glitter covered the balance of the wax.

All of the candles in this picture are simple to make and all use large amounts of whipped wax, but the end results are completely different.

Valentine, Easter, and Christmas
GINGERBREAD CANDLES

Another way to get rid of leftover wax is to throw all scraps back in the melting pot and add as much brown dye as necessary to get either a gingerbread color or a chocolate brown.

Pour wax into a greased pan to a depth of at least one inch, and when the wax is firm, cut out Christmas cookie shapes such as a tree, star, gingerbread man, and so on. A wick hole can be made with a hot ice pick, or two shapes the same size can be fastened together with hot wax. If this is done, place a wick along the center of one half before fastening the two sides together.

With a cake decorating tool or pastry cone, put Whip Wax 'icing' on the cookie candles.

8
Profiles in Wax

SANDY LEMLER

Sandy Lemler of Hawaiian Gardens, California, is the owner of Candles of Distinction and is an old pro with about eighteen years of candlemaking experience behind him. Sandy started with candles when it wasn't possible to run to the hobby shop for a package of dye or sit down and make up an order to an out of town supplier. In those days he experimented with the few samples that could be located after months of searching and repeatedly trying different formulas and combinations until the best possible one could be found.

Sandy says constant research is a part of his past but is also part of his present and future. He has never stopped his researching, analyzing, and experimenting, and probably never will. The results of this continuing effort are candles of distinction. Quality is the prime requisite for Sandy's candles.

This candlemaker has a background in art which began in Manly, Iowa. His interest in art was encouraged by his sister and also by an artist friend from the Minneapolis Art Institute. He still remembers his first carving, which was a statue of a Japanese woman after the Hiroshima devastation. Although Sandy has worked with many phases of art, he has always returned to candlemaking and finds it more satisfying than any other medium. However, this knowledge of various art forms has proved invaluable in his candlemaking, not only from a design standpoint, but in the blending of his colors and oils.

An article in a craft magazine about two ladies who had produced a candle that burned only in the center and glowed, the original glo-

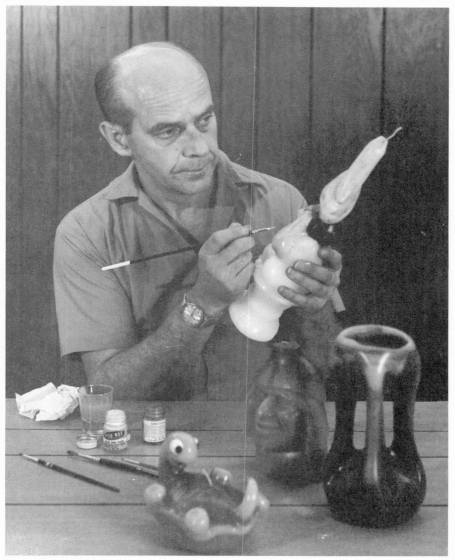

Illustration No. 68. *Sandy Lemler painting detail on his candles.*

candle, was the beginning of his involvement with wax and wicks. After that he was on his own because, other than a Chevron research booklet, he found no information on candles for a long time. Several years ago, while in a veterans' hospital, he discovered some books and articles in

Illustration No. 69. *More of Sandy's candles.*

the library which were helpful, but by then he had scratched for most of his information the hard way.

No dedicated candlecrafter can ever pass up a possible opportunity to learn something new about the craft. With this in mind, Sandy signed up for the Candle Institute course. He says that even with all of his working experience of candlemaking, he still gained new knowledge from this course. After completing the course and obtaining the state-approved certificate, which is a requisite for all their staff, he began doing consultation work for them. From there he went into design and testing and is now the Chief Consultant and Technical Adviser. Sometimes he will spend as much as three days in research to be able to answer the question of a single student.

He credits Mr. Fred Dunn, a retired chemist, with his continuing research and quest for knowledge. Never one to feel his store of knowledge is complete, Sandy is always ready to listen and eager to learn. Also, for anyone exhibiting a sincere interest in candlemaking, he will do all he can to help him.

The staff of Candles of Distinction is well trained in candlemaking, and all of them are attuned to Sandy's insistence on quality. No seconds ever knowingly leave his plant. Although Candles of Distinction makes a full line of candles, the specialty is scents. Over 160 essential oils are included in the company's extensive stock. These scents are custom blended for the individual customer, and Sandy will even blend a shade or color to complement the scent. This attention to detail and insistence on only the best has brought him loyal customers from a nine-state area.

In addition to holding down a part-time job and running his own candle company, Mr. Lemler is also the hard-working Treasurer of Chandlers International. He claims that the quality craftsmanship of the members of this candle guild gives him an added incentive to keep on improving his own line.

Another of his duties for the Candle Institute, in addition to being Chief Consultant and Technical Adviser, is writing an article each month for their candle publication "Fun and Profit Hobbies." Any one of these things would be all that most people could handle, but Sandy also corresponds on a regular basis with his many candlemaking friends throughout the world.

Sandy effectively demolishes the myth that candlemaking is a nice pastime for sweet little old ladies, but certainly not a craft that a man would find interesting. Besides all the good things it can be, candlemaking can be hard and tiring work.

JEAN WINKLER

In 1959 Jean Winkler's family was growing up and leaving home for careers and marriage, and she decided it would be necessary to do something to fill the gap. She had made almost everything there was to be made for the essentials of rearing a family, and she wanted to do something pretty and non-essential for a change of pace.

While trying to collect everything needed to make poured candles, she discovered the honeycomb beeswax sheets. It seemed incredible to her that a candle could be made from a sheet of wax, but she was intrigued. Also, her spare time was still limited, and the beeswax candles could be completed in a short time. She says the result was that she more or less "rolled her way into the candle business."

By 1964 the business had grown so much that a shop and storeroom had to be built. Managing their candle business is now a full time job for Jean and Don Winkler, and when she can spare the time, their daughter also helps them. Jean says this sounds like the perfect cooperative family enterprise, but actually the rest of the family is "livestock-minded" and would prefer doing something else.

Jean purchases the supplies, makes all the candles, and does some selling. Don does the butting and polishing, most of the selling, and all of the packaging. They also have an additional line of finished driftwood pieces, mostly candle holders. The unique part of their business is the fact that they live on a dairy farm which is twelve miles from the nearest town of 5,000 people. However, they are on a state highway leading to a resort area.

She took her beeswax candles to the neighboring county fairs for five successive summers and feels this is one of the worst places to merchandise candles. However, there were advantages because some of the customers she met there are still buying her candles. She also met people who helped her locate sources of supplies, which was no small problem back in those days. Jean is particularly grateful to Don Olsen of Pourette Mfg. Co. for his patience and help when she was trying to decide whether to go into the candle supply business.

In 1961 at one of the fairs, she heard about the Candle Institute course and used the money earned at the fair to enroll in the course. From that she learned the fundamentals of candlemaking and began pouring molded candles.

Probably the most unusual feature of the Winkler's candle business is the making of gypsy candles for the Servian Christmas which is celebrated from January 19th through the 21st. The candles are made for one of the largest gypsy tribes in the United States. Candles are the core of the gypsy religion and celebration and are decorated accordingly. The celebration is begun with a feast and the lighting of candles.

In Illustration No. 70 the two outside candles and middle-of-the-center candle are made from a roll of one-fourth of an inch thick smooth

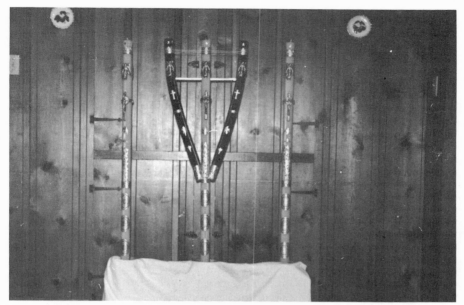

Illustration No. 70. *Gypsy candle for Servian Christmas.*

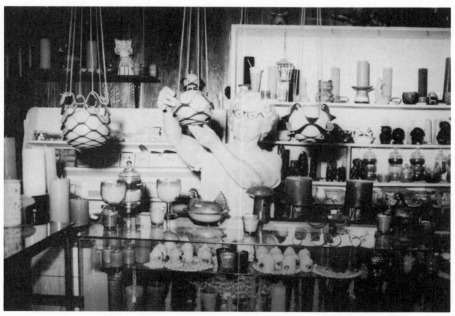

Illustration No. 71. *Jean Winkler hanging a candle in her shop.*

beeswax and then covered with honeycomb sheets. The arms on the center candle were made from red honeycomb beeswax. The symbols on the candle are wax figurines and gold foil medallions. From top to bottom

Illustration No. 72. *A corner of the Winklers' candle shop.*

is an angel with wings, Christ on the Cross, and gold medallions, representing the Garden of Eden. This candle was made for the King of the Gypsies and is five feet tall and three inches in diameter. The King always celebrates, and generally, his mother and his brothers celebrate also.

The gypsy traditions are handed down through the tribes from the European culture. In Europe, a tribe's religion is governed, to some extent, by the territory in which it lives. Here the King tries to keep the religion and the blood lines intact.

Often the bride and groom never have a courtship. The father chooses a bride for his son, and a ceremony takes place, but no legal marriage certificate is used. If the couple is not compatible, the father-in-law pays the bride's father to take her back, and the bride's father, in turn, resells her.

Jean says all phases of candlemaking and her business have been challenging, stimulating, enlightening, good mental and physical therapy, and lucrative. It has also been exhausting, discouraging, and exasperating, which seems to be the formula for any successful business enterprise.

MARGARET L. HOSFORD

Margaret Hosford of Englewood, Colorado, has been interested in candlemaking since 1950 when she carved her first Tiki candle as a gift for her husband. She still has this first effort in her candle collection.

As she became more interested in making candles as well as carving them, she found there was little information available to a beginner. Sources of supplies and material for making candles were limited. For a long time, the only wax formula she could locate was one for tallow wax candles, and this she found in a 1909 cookbook. Later she ran across a formula for composition wax candles in a book called "Henley's Formulas," but this book was published in 1926, and she was positive that somewhere there was later information available. Thus, she began her search for information about waxes, where they came from, and what they did. Even now, a part of each day is devoted to research on this fascinating project. Someday she plans to compile all this research into one article or book and share it with all candlemakers.

In spite of the time spent researching, it was not until 1955 when Humble Oil Company opened a branch office in her hometown of Enid, Oklahoma, that she received any expert help with waxes. She contacted them soon after they opened their office, and they were generous with information on their waxes and helped her contact other oil companies for information about their waxes. A short time later, her brother went to work for a crayon company, and soon he and their chemists were helping her locate suitable oil dyes and other additives for her candles.

Just about the time she had solved most of her wax and dye problems, a friend sent her a Candle Institute ad. She enrolled and received her first instruction on candlemaking and her first professional molds. In 1964 she wrote her first candlemaking article for *Fun and Profit Hobbies,* and in 1969 she became Editor and Art Director for the publication. Since that time, she has had several candlemaking articles published in craft magazines.

Margaret has appeared on many TV programs demonstrating the art of candlemaking, has taught this craft in several states, and was sponsored by the Enid Artists League in several one-man candle shows. During the years she lived in Enid, she also made all the candles for the annual candle show sponsored by the Central National Bank and Trust Company. She has won several first prizes for her candles at candle shows, and for candle and bases at ceramic shows. She designs many of her own candles and makes most of her own molds.

This candlemaker's father says the early training she received in his bakery, starting to decorate cakes and cookies at age 4, was responsible

Illustration No. 73. *Margaret attaching wax angels to a pillar candle.*

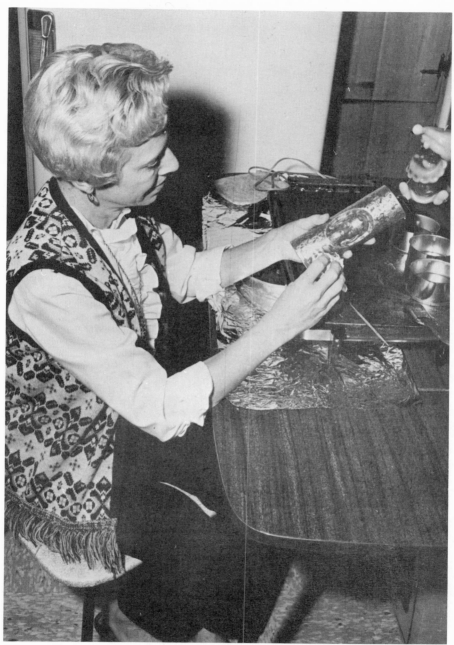

Illustration No. 74. *Margaret Hosford at her worktable, putting the finishing touches on a Christmas candle.*

Illustration No. 75. *A jolly little Santa poured in two colors.*

for her ability to decorate candles. However, we imagine that her art training and interest in all arts and crafts was helpful.

Margaret's interest in candlemaking was kept on a hobby basis for several years. However, in 1960 she opened the first Candlelite House in Enid, Oklahoma, and in 1967 opened a second shop in Kansas, and in 1969 a third one in California. The second and third shops were in partnership with two of her sisters, and now a fourth shop is opening in California in partnership with her nephew.

Until her husband died in 1968, Margaret combined candlemaking with a career in insurance, managing insurance agencies and teaching insurance at the University of Oklahoma. Since 1968 she has devoted all her time to candlemaking interests, which include being Secretary of Chandlers International as well as the writing, research, and candlemaking mentioned earlier.

Between the time that this book was written and the edited manuscript came back for checking, Margaret joined the staff of the Aloha Candle Company in Hawaii as Production Manager and Director of Research.

Appendix

WHERE TO BUY

Because of the difficulty often encountered in finding the necessary supplies for making and decorating candles, the Supplier Listing below is offered to make the search easier. Some of these firms have a small charge for their catalogs, and all of them would appreciate receiving a stamped, self-addressed envelope along with your inquiry.

GENERAL CANDLEMAKING SUPPLIES

Pourette Mfg. Co.
6818 Roosevelt Way N.E.
Seattle, Washington 98115

The Candle Mill
East Arlington, Vermont 05252

Town & Country Crafts
235 Turnpike
Pequannock, New Jersey 07440

Fitzgerald Enterprises, Inc.
P. O. Box 2095
Oakland, California 94604

KaPat Candle Products
P. O. Box 5413
Irving, Texas 75060

The Burning Candle
400 Littleton Road
Parsippany, New Jersey 07054

Village Candle Store
Box 486
Marshfield, Wisconsin 54449

Cake Decorators
Blacklick, Ohio 43004

SCENTS

Candles of Distinction
12426 E. 223 St.
Hawaiian Gardens, Calif. 90716

Paul & Gordon Wagner
4025 Glenwick Lane
Dallas, Texas 75205

Farrand Chemical Co.
Box 39
Tyrone, Pa. 16686

148

Natcol Crafts, Inc.
32074 Dunlap Blvd.
Yucaipa, California 92399

Hawthorne House, Inc.
103 North Robinson St.
Bloomington, Illinois 61701

Supreme Handicrafts
Box 395
Sioux Falls, South Dakota 57101

Glo-Candle Co.
Box 10102
Kansas City, Missouri 64111

Louisa Candle Supply
250 Clayton St.
Denver, Colorado 80206

Celebration
Box 28
Pentwater, Michigan 49449

Candles & Supplies by Doll
921 West Collins Ave.
Orange, California 92667

PAINTS

Markal Company
250 N. Washtenaw Ave.
Chicago, Illinois 60612

TISSUE PAPER

Austen Display Corporation
133 West 19th St.
New York, N.Y. 10011

DYE (Bulk)

Pylan Products
95–10 218 St.
Queens Village, N.Y.

Keystone Aniline & Dye Corp.
321 N. Loomis St.
Chicago, Illinois 60607

PLASTIC CRYSTALS

Eastman Chemical Products
Kingsport, Tennessee 37660
(Epolene N-10)

FOREIGN SUPPLIERS

This listing is for the convenience of candlemakers living in these countries. The red tape, import duty, and high shipping costs would make it impractical for citizens of the U.S. to consider buying any of their supplies overseas.

Lumi-Craft (Canada) Ltd.
P.O. Box 666
Kingston, Ontario, Canada

Camp-O-Matic Ltd.
P. O. Box 21
Lansdowne
Capetown, South Africa

Carberry Candles
Carberry
Musselburgh
Midlothian
Scotland

Index